TI

An image typical of
the Ardennes: open
countryside and low
hills between forests
and valleys.

BATTLES IN FOCUS

THE ARDENNES
The Battle of the Bulge

J. MARK CONNELL

BRASSEY'S

First published in 2003 by Brassey's

A member of Chrysalis Books plc

Brassey's
The Chrysalis Building, Bramley Road,
London W10 6SP

North American orders:
Casemate Publishing, 2114 Darby Road,
Havertown, PA 19083, USA

J. Mark Connell has asserted his moral right
to be identified as the author of this work.

Library of Congress Cataloging in Publication Data
available

British Library Cataloguing in Publication Data
A catalogue record for this book is available
from the British Library

ISBN 1 85753 323 2

All photographs: Chrysalis Images

Edited and designed by DAG Publications Ltd
Designed by David Gibbons
Edited by Michael Boxall
Cartography by Anthony A. Evans

Cover illustration courtesy John Batchelor

Printed in Spain.

CONTENTS

INTRODUCTION

The World War of 1939–45 had almost run its course. The German nation, led by the belligerent dictates of Adolf Hitler, had tested the resolve of the European people to the north, west and south and the cohesiveness of the block of assorted nations and traditions to the east. It had found initial success easy to achieve by employing a dramatic new military strategy employing the newest weaponry of the day in a combination that was 'blitzkrieg'.

Those who sought to stand in the way of German expansionism had not applied themselves to the study of future warfare during the years of peace following the 1914–18 conflict. On the other hand, Germany, supposedly prevented by the Versailles Treaty from re-arming, *had* kept their Great War practitioners in war colleges and schools of the military art where they had planned and considered, evaluated and examined. The 'blitzkrieg' philosophy had emerged from this source and put the Germans on the front foot in 1939.

Because of their inertia, those who fought against the early German thrusts did not stand a chance. Forces armed with old weaponry and outdated theories were incapable of delaying, let alone stopping, the German advance through the Ardennes and across Belgium into France, and the supplementary units rushed from Britain were no better prepared. Hitler's Third Reich had been poised to invade Britain when the latter's air arm showed resolve and courage beyond the call of duty to dent German enthusiasm and cause Hitler to switch hostilities to the Eastern Front.

The once covert support Britain had enjoyed from the United States was now brought more into the open. Active participation was now assured, and accentuated by the attack on Pearl Harbor and Hitler's rash declaration of war against the USA. Now the united resources of the expanded Allied forces – its political, manufacturing and manpower strengths – were always likely to hold sway and, if the plans to take the war back to the Reich were somewhat tortuous and fraught with debilitating argument and prevarication, there was sufficient focus to maintain momentum.

Adolf Hitler, his nose now bloodied in the East, could not prevent the Normandy landings, though his Army fought hard to prevent the breakout of Allied forces from the region. Once he had failed in this he chose to retreat back to his national boundaries with only modest attempts made to stall the Allied march across France. To most observers the next great battle would be for German territory with the Führer fortifying the natural boundary of the Siegfried Line with every man and machine he could. His ability to do this would, in the views of the Allied planners, be substantially reduced by virtue of the debilitating Allied bombing campaign that had surely decimated German industry and demoralised the people. It would only be a matter of time before Hitler's Germany would be overrun and the Führer driven from power.

Such thinking ignored various important factors. Firstly, dictators do not act in a routine way, especially when cornered and facing humiliation; they do not go quietly. Secondly, the German military manufacture was not in as parlous a state as the Allies thought, and, thirdly, the German military, whilst in many instances disillusioned and disenchanted with its political leadership, retained a strong sense of national pride and duty. There was also the element that the majority of German nationals were still supportive of the war despite the awesome damage being caused to their towns and factories by Allied bombing action.

In truth, there had been an element of Hitler drawing the Allied armies on to him. Though his forces had fought long and hard for the Channel ports they held, elsewhere many units had moved back to the German border with almost indecent haste. There was considerable debate in Allied command about whether too large a gap had been allowed to form between their formations and the retreating Germans. This was all part of Hitler's evolving plan, desperate and ill-considered though it was, for he had said at the time of the Allied landings that his planners should get ready for a counter-attack in the winter months. Then,

Below: German troops attack around an artillery-damaged American position.

he said, the weather conditions would reduce the enemy's air superiority and give advantage to German ground troops more used to their home terrain; there was also the chance of long-promised 'super' weapons coming on stream.

All military sense and established practice, let alone sound political thinking, suggested the Führer's priority should have been to show strong defensive resistance and prosecute for the best peace he could achieve. This strange man, however, having shown himself capable of grandiose bravado and occasional intuitive thinking, now collapsed into manic and ill-considered directives that were foolish and bad for his nation. And yet, amidst error-strewn and poorly conceived scheming he still managed to show some flashes of brilliance.

Firstly, his choice to counter-attack had no chance of success unless he secured absolute surprise. He knew this, prized it and achieved it. Secondly, he multiplied the level of surprise by choosing a route of attack completely unexpected by his opponents, and whether we deem this to have been stubborn or astute, it certainly added to Allied confusion. Thirdly, he secured amazing numbers of men and weaponry with which to mount his attack. The Allies were always going to be able to outnumber him and his generals were going to waste men and machines through bad tactics but he still produced a vast force considering the months of reverse he had experienced. Fourthly, he even had the awareness to label his campaign with words that suggested the defensive build-up the Allies were expecting rather than the offensive he was planning.

The Ardennes Offensive brought to the battlefield the largest force of American army personnel seen to that point, it stretched Allied accord to the limit and it came within a few hundred yards of achieving at least its initial objective of crossing the River Meuse. The short campaign saw diverse action in treacherous conditions where many of Hitler's personal predictions came true, only for further success to be lost to poor decision-making on his part and some of his battlefield generals.

The war was already lost when Hitler mounted 'Wacht am Rhein' but it was somewhat more than a foolish death-throe. His military advisers – men of considerable experience – were against the scheme and the force of men he sent on the mission contained too few with proven battle-zone skills. Within a larger war, however, the Battle for the Ardennes – an area more likely to be chosen for military exercise than a forward offensive – featured almost every land warfare tactic and merits study for that reason alone. That it was also the severest live action test of the Allied political and military leadership, and its failure removed any chance of significant defence of their homeland by the losers, means that it is one of the most significant periods of the Second World War.

The aim of this book is to discuss the constituent parts of the Battle of the Bulge and to consider the reasoning behind the German move. It will seek to demonstrate why, amidst a World War lasting almost six years, these thirty days of fighting in a minor European country remain avidly studied by general and military historians alike.

1

THE WAR IN WESTERN EUROPE
THE SITUATION ON 15 DECEMBER 1944

Once the Allies had broken out of Normandy and retaken Paris, their drive towards the German border had been chiefly devoid of tough fighting. Just 193 days after the D-Day landings they were closing in on their target with the expectation of fierce battles at the 'West Wall' (Siegfried Line) when they attempted a full breakthrough, though all the evidence was that the much weakened and retreating enemy could be overcome.

At this point, however, there had been some disappointing hitches. There had been some dispute, and certainly much debate, as to how the Allied armies should progress to and across the German border with Montgomery and Bradley among the senior commanders pressing for narrow thrusts while Eisenhower, Supreme Commander of the entire Allied land force from September, insisting on a broader line of advance. The subsequent push to Antwerp by Montgomery had not been entirely successful – the city was reached in early September but the port and access to the sea were not secured until early November. The attempt to secure key river and canal bridges in Holland, and thus open a route around the northern end of the German defensive lines, had been damaged by the failure at Arnhem. These were the first major reversals in what had been an extraordinarily successful operation since the Normandy landings.

The need to secure the Channel ports to the east of the invasion beaches had been acknowledged very early in the planning of the campaign; they would be vital to keep forward progress supplied. Although the Allied front-line troops had left Paris behind them before the end of August and were at Brussels by 3 September, the ports of Le Havre – more than 300 miles to the *west* of the Belgian capital – St-Valery and Dieppe were not taken until mid-September. The vital port of Antwerp was taken on 4 September, but the advance forces were unable to force the Germans out of the Scheldt Estuary between the port and the sea.

The failure to secure the use of Antwerp was a major blow. Eisenhower had made it clear to Montgomery that it was crucial to the Allied advance to and across the Rhine so all parties were aware that failure here would bring a reluctance to attempt a crossing of the German border.

Such was the strength of the German positions in the Scheldt estuary and on the islands there that it was to take almost twelve weeks from the Allies setting foot in the city before they could claim it as an operational supply-point and the first convoy was able to reach the port. These months of delay limited the ambitions of Eisenhower and the planners; there were no significant forward moves in the north and centre of the Allied front, although the impatient Patton, supported by 6 Army Group arriving from the south, did edge beyond the Moselle.

In anticipation of having the port available within weeks, Eisenhower had already issued orders at the end of October that the primary route into Germany would be to the north in order that the industrial heartland of the enemy could be put out of action and the supply lines to the Allied front line would remain short. The advance towards Berlin would continue when and where he chose; the enemy, he imagined, would be too weak to mount any significant counter-attack. But their spirited resistance in the Scheldt could not be described as timid, and it seemed likely that they would put up a stout defence of their country.

The delay at Antwerp meant that the West Wall remained effectively intact and a significant asset for the Germans. Furthermore, their infrastructure and the will of the people was still good despite the work of Allied aircraft against factories, transport systems and city centres. In this the German people were proving as resolute as had the British when the roles were reversed. So at this point Hitler could reasonably quote reasons for continuing the fight, and consider doing so on the front foot rather than the back.

The loss of Antwerp was as bad for the Germans as it was beneficial to the Allies. Had his generals held on, as he had insisted, Hitler's options could have been more attractive, his actions more positive. In his eyes the situation was poor but not yet beyond saving; he was certainly refusing to countenance any political moves or negotiations.

For many months Hitler had been planning a counter-attack, and it had always been his intention that it should be through the Ardennes. The pause in the Allied advance had given him the 'window of opportunity' he needed. If it were possible to persuade him to make political decisions to end the war satisfactorily, he would far rather do so during or just after a battlefield success. He had told his military chiefs in August that, though he hated it, it was necessary to wait, and then make the right moves at a time that suited them. His recovery of Antwerp might sow dissent and disillusionment in the opposition ranks, and in any event his position would be very much better than at present.

There have been plenty of military leaders who have chosen to counter-attack when all seemed lost. For reasons based on sound military strategy, but more often out of desperation, commanders-in-chief have ordered one final effort from troops on the cusp of defeat, not just a 'last stand' but a surprise offensive that will catch those expecting victory unawares. Some – though very few – of these gambles have been successful.

Hitler's senior military commanders were advising him to shore up the West Wall, hold the Allied advance, and negotiate, but he could not accept this. They had been similarly reluctant just thirty-eight months before when he had pushed his forces westwards to a point where they had been poised to conquer the British; more recently German troops had been on the doorstep of Moscow. From those positions, negotiations had not been part of the plan; anything other than victory had not been discussed. The Führer regularly reminded his generals how the glory and reputations they gained for their 'Blitzkrieg years' were due to his own insistence on implementing the plan; he taunted them about their initial apathy and asserted that anyone could have achieved their result with him as their leader. There was every reason, in his mind, to try the same route and the same policy again for his achievements in 1939–40 had also fuelled his low opinion of Allied generalship, a view his advisers could not change even though the arrival of the USA into the war, the Allied landings in France and the debilitating reversals in the east had left Germany bloodied and all but bowed.

It was the prize of Antwerp that was filling Hitler's mind in the autumn of 1944 for he had seen how desperately the Allies had fought for it, could understand how it would now fuel their confidence and, above all, recalled how his beloved 'Blitzkrieg' techniques had swept him to the city once before, *en route* to greater goals in 1940.

So was it solely the memory of that successful thrust through the Ardennes that prompted him towards a repeat performance? There have been almost as many theories as historians writing on the episode. Only a very few colleagues were party to the Führer's increasingly manic thinking at this stage of the war, but these were the options being considered by him and his closest advisers at the time:

1 He truly believed there was a dispute in the Allied ranks and that even a minor setback could cause it to broaden.
2 He remained unconvinced that the Americans had the heart for a European land fight and that, again, a reversal of fortunes in battle could bring this to a head.
3 His only chance of victory from the parlous position in which he found himself would come if the advanced weaponry he had been investing in for so long would finally prove operational. With every day that passed, however, he was receiving reports of more delays because of lack of equipment and raw materials, bombed factories, and disillusioned workers. Delaying the Allied advance, causing opposition commanders to have second thoughts about crossing into Germany, could earn him valuable time.
4 For the above reason, and for his continuing war effort, he desperately needed fuel and there were vast stores in Allied hands in Belgium.
5 The Soviets were threatening a breakthrough in the Danube valley. An attack on the Anglo-American thrust might cause the Soviets to rethink the wisdom of this move, even to begin negotiations for settlement.
6 The Allied advance had paused to re-equip and plan for a spring offensive. Although his troops had bad memories of fighting in a freezing Russia, Hitler knew that they would be more at home in an Ardennes winter than either the British or Americans.
7 He was aware that the forests, hills and valleys of the Ardennes were a weakly defended section of the Allied front line, because the Allied commanders

could not conceive of any offensive action, by either side, being mounted across such unsuitable terrain.

8 Antwerp – the ultimate target of the counter-offensive – was a vital element of the Allied supply route and a prized asset for either side (though Hitler seemed to be concentrating on its capture and the effect it would have on Allied morale rather than what he would do with it once it was in his hands).

9 He was confident that he could conceal his preparations and so have surprise on his side.

It can be debated whether any of these thoughts were realistic, but Hitler was not to be swayed from his long-standing plan for a strike through the heart of the Ardennes.

He knew what overall defeat would mean – although his assertion that 'if the war is to be lost, the nation will also perish' was the strident view of an egotist – but he spoke of it to very few. His public pronouncements remained confident in their expression of ultimate victory though he was increasingly expressing, especially to military commanders in the field, the need to delay the Allied advance. He presented such calls as temporary solutions that would bring reward in terms of the much-promised new weapons and, he assured every listener, nervousness among the opposition.

The German Army had spent months retreating on the Eastern and Western Fronts, its navy had been almost unseen for a year, and the Luftwaffe was being mauled every time it attempted more than bland support of the withdrawal. From such a wretched state it would take blind indifference to the circumstances, unwarranted optimism in one's own destiny or, perhaps, an ability to see the one remaining chink in the enemy's armour, even to consider the path Hitler was to choose. One has to remember that if he was not a skilled, tutored and experienced military technician, he was an instinctive dictator whose strategies had enjoyed nothing but success until the previous few months. He entertained no criticism, accepted few counter arguments and was constantly attended by sycophants and servants.

Militarily he had, until recently, always been the one who attacked; he was also more likely to revert to methods that had worked in the past than to employ complex military defensive strategies freshly planned on charts and blackboards. He claimed always to favour offensive tactics, and was determined to avoid the static attritional warfare of 1914–18.

At the same time, there was an element in his thinking that favoured the idea of drawing the Allies on to a position where they would be vulnerable to counter-attack. At a meeting with his closest associates in mid-August, when the Allies had just burst through the German defences at Falaise, he was warning them to be prepared to take the offensive in November when weather conditions would ensure that enemy aircraft would be less effective; he was surely imagining then that by that time the Allies would be still be in the ascendancy and that, after a long, tiring advance, they would be susceptible to a counter-strike in the tough winter conditions.

While he was still calling for every scrap of occupied territory to be fought for, the German leader was also ordering heavy defensive reinforcement of the West Wall and on other fronts so as to be able to launch his counter from a position of strength. On 4 September, as the Allies first took Antwerp, the veteran General Field Marshal Gerd von Rundstedt was recalled to the post of Commander-in-Chief West to create the defensive line that would bring the Allied forces to a halt and give Hitler his chance to strike. The general was required to stop the Allies at the Albert Canal and the Meuse, but before he had reached the front to supervise the work, the enemy was encamped beyond that line and only the Upper Moselle section of the proposed 'new defensive line' was held, and then only by using troops reserved for the proposed new offensive.

To achieve Hitler's aim, von Rundstedt believed that he needed six weeks and some 2,000 tanks and ten more infantry divisions. He knew he would not get them, of course, so he did what he could with meagre resources and succeeded in limiting the Allied gains. Although they crossed the Meuse on 8 September and were on German soil four days later, the Allies suffered for lack of a clear aim at this point. It was not so much that von Rundstedt out-thought the forward Allied commanders or that his defences were very effective, but more that the Allies had allowed the retreating German troops to drift too far ahead of them, and were holding a front line of such width that at no point could they muster sufficient numbers to break through and pursue. Some contend, German commanders and historians among them, that the war would have ended months earlier had Eisenhower concentrated his men for a greater forward thrust at this time.

With impasse at the West Wall, Hitler was able to consider how to draw together the necessary forces and equipment to mount his planned offensive in the Ardennes. He had long since been using too many men and too much of his diminishing equipment on other fronts in the west, east or in Italy, and to protect U-boat bases in the western Baltic because he deemed it important to keep these open for the promised new vessels that would be part of the next attacking phase. There were also many divisions out of circulation in the eastern Baltic lands, more in Hungary and Austria and others in Yugoslavia and Scandinavia. It was about now that it might have occurred to the German leader that he had fought too long on too many fronts, protecting diminishing assets and failing to move troops to where they were most needed; the problem had exercised greater minds than his among his predecessors.

Nevertheless, there was no evidence of a lack of support from the bulk of the German people in supporting a continuing war effort, especially in the armament and munitions factories that the Allies had tried so hard to render useless. Remarkably, there were more single-engined aircraft built in September 1944 (3,031) than in any other month of the year.[1] This outstanding production performance, masterminded by Hitler's miracle-worker Albert Speer, was only part of the massive manufacturing effort conjured up in support of the Führer's 'last fling'. There were nearly 1,000 tanks a month being produced at this time together with 170,000 rifles, 27,000 machine-guns, 1,000 anti-tank guns, more than 2,000 mortars, 1,500 other guns and some 321,000 tons of ammunition. It was an astonishing replenishment programme, and even fuel was made available by dint of frugal use within Germany and a lessening of Allied air strikes as the weather worsened. If only he could have produced more soldiers and pilots with similar efficiency!

On the matter of personnel, Heinrich Himmler had managed to create 25 Volksgrenadier divisions by calling up every last fit man, young or old, skilled or unskilled, in a desperate mobilisation. A determined nation-wide policy, operated by Goebbels, rounded up more than 500,000 men from factories and colleges, and from the air and naval forces, with scant regard for whether any amount of short-term training could turn them into an adequate fighting force. The new Sixth Panzer Army was a different matter in that, although drawing on Volksgrenadier divisions, it boasted paratroop units and special forces as well as four SS Panzer divisions.

It was a major illusion on Hitler's part, however, to pretend to the German people that these numbers meant fresh military might that could change national fortunes. Although the Germans had not been so ruthless in recruiting every able-bodied person for military service as propagandists claim, the new force was not as efficient as it could have been; in the interest of numerical strength raw recruits were taking the place of battle-hardened soldiers who could have been combed out and returned to the front. It is estimated that, from 1 June to 1 September 1944, the Germans had lost in excess of 1.2 million dead, wounded or missing, and more were surrounded by enemy advances. Of equal concern, despite the manufacturing impetus, was that tanks and other fighting vehicles were being lost by the hour.

Hitler had always maintained there were two outcomes possible from his expansionist adventures since 1939: he could succeed, or he could fail. In the middle of December 1944 he was poised to take a last gamble to achieve the former result. The Allied front line had now pushed forward to a point where, for most of its length, it abutted the West Wall defences; in many locations the combatants were within rifle range of one another, and casual observation of the enemy's daily life was the chief entertainment for the sentries during this relatively quiet period. Only east of Aachen and in a small sector below the Schnee Eifel had the Allies driven beyond the fortified zone. The section of the Wall through which the German offensive would be conducted stretched from just north of Echternach, twenty miles north-east of the city of Luxembourg, to a little north of Monschau, a town some fifteen miles south of Aachen, a recently acquired Allied prize.

From Echternach the Allied front line – manned by troops of 4th Infantry Division in Major General Middleton's VIII Corps – followed the River Sauer across from the cliffs on its eastern bank. A few miles further on 9th Armored Division was on patrol but, recently arrived in Europe, it had still not got all its personnel up to these the most forward locations. From the point where the River Our joined the Sauer, 28th Infantry Division took over and it, like the 4th, was supposed to be resting after the bitter battles fought in the Hürtgen Forest in November. The gorges formed by these rivers were the reason the Siegfried Line had been sited here; there were few crossings and certainly none suitable for large formations. A natural line of defence and difficult to penetrate from west to east, it was, by definition, not ideal for launching a massed advance through to the west.

The front continued north through Vianden to the point, fifteen miles beyond, where gains made on the other side of the Wall had produced a salient which the 28th held until 106th Infantry Division took over at Oberhausen. This was another recently arrived group and they had been told to expect a quiet life by the troops of V Corps' 2nd Infantry Division whom they replaced. The next handover was to 99th Infantry Division, also of Major General Leonard Gerow's V Corps, and at this junction the front was at its most weak in terms of numbers. At the precise point where Middleton's VIII Corps transferred control of the front to Gerow, at the northern edge of the Losheim Gap, there was a vacant two-mile stretch where there were no manned defences at all, not a tank, not a foxhole, and German defenders reportedly walked through here without let or hindrance to visit family homes behind enemy lines.[2]

Farther north again, the 99th's defences were interjected by an offensive action being undertaken by units of 2nd Division who had gone north to attempt a narrow breakthrough towards the Roer Dams, just twenty or so miles into enemy territory. Beyond there the 99th took charge again through to the border town of Monschau.

This was not a simple battle front from which to launch an invasion of Germany. From the security of its natural barriers, the Germans had made attacks to the west three times before, in 1870, 1914 and 1940; now they were to drive forward again, but this time as a result of desperate dictates from a deluded leader.

Below: US artillery during the battle for Bastogne.

2
PREPARATIONS

Although we have seen that Hitler had long been planning a counter-offensive in the autumn of 1944 and had set matters of equipment production and troop recruitment in hand as early as the summer, it was not until 16 September that the scheme was first announced, albeit to the small group of his privileged advisers. He must have been longing to see how these men would react to his ideas, eager to reverse the litany of bad news that took up the daily meetings, but whether he actually planned disclosure on this September morning we shall never know. Certainly he was showing impatience as Alfred Jodl began his briefing for the Führer, Wilhelm Keitel, Werner Kreipe – Chief of Staff for OKL (Luftwaffe High Command) and representing Göring, and, unusually, Heinz Guderian. The report made mention, in muted tones and words devoid of emotion, of the present strengths of the combatants including a further ten divisions presently *en route* from England to the north-west European theatre, before moving on to the vexed topic of shortages of tanks, weapons and ammunition cramping the plans of the German commanders. Then, as Jodl sought to move swiftly on to the situation in the south of France, Hitler violently interjected with a statement that was both strident and succinct. 'I have just made a momentous decision. I shall go over to the counter-attack, that is to say' and pointing to the large map on the table around which the group were sitting, 'here, out of the Ardennes, with the objective … Antwerp!'

No-one dared to comment – this was a time to stay silent. The Führer outlined his plans, the thinking that was to galvanise the armed forces of the Third Reich into a new forward move after months of painful and frustrating withdrawal and retreat. The nation was virtually without allies, was facing a combined Allied force that could out-number and out-spend it, and should have surely been looking to push for as positive a negotiated settlement as it could. But this is the view of history rather than that of a desperate dictator who still held beliefs and expectations, however unreasonable these might be.

Adolf Hitler had few of the assets required by a military commander. He had been an avid reader of military history and admired the warrior leaders of the past, such as Frederick the Great, whose picture hung in his office and whose oath to the flag was featured in that taken by aspiring SS officers, but his belief in his own strategic and tactical thinking was naive and ill-founded; his talent was superficial and his decisions driven by weak theories and sudden impulse. He is, however, entitled to some credit for three things relating to his move in the Ardennes: first, it was based on the worthy advantage gained by surprise – in both location and timing; second, there *was* some disquiet in the Allied ranks but not at the level he chose to believe; and third, the American troops who had been so important in the Allied drive out of France had not been tested by major setbacks for some time.

We know that Hitler had told his senior generals to be ready for an autumn offensive as early as the time when the Allies were breaking out of Normandy, but little is known about how much detailed planning took place between then and his outburst on 16 September, though we can believe that he had other matters on his mind around 20 July when he survived the bomb plot by disillusioned generals.

There had long been a specified need to protect the industrial heartland of Germany, especially the Ruhr, with Hitler admitting to his fears in November 1943 when he opined that the threat in the east was 'outweighed by the threat from the west where enemy success would strike immediately at the heart of the German war economy'. Even though the Reich had not been bombed into submission by the Allied air raids, and the output of the Ruhr factories remained remarkably high, Hitler must have seen that an Allied land advance into Germany via that route would be a terminal blow, nationally and personally.

He had forgone an 'Ardennes-type' initiative in the east because, rightly or wrongly, he felt it more likely that he could find a political settlement with the Stalin regime that bore many of the traits of his own power base. From his position in the late summer of 1944 he could not fight on two major fronts, certainly could not find the wherewithal to drive through to the west and still be active in the east.

One month after the failed bomb plot, it appears Hitler had made up his mind. On 19 August he told Speer and Walter Buhle, the latter being Chief of Staff at OKW (Armed Forces High Command), to create large numbers of men and *matériel* for the Western Front and, though it was a further month before he disclosed his attack route to others, this must have been part of his preparations. For the next few weeks, while urging territory to be retained at all costs and no backwards steps be taken, the Führer remained chiefly calm as bad news followed day after day – another indication that his thoughts were centred on a grand riposte – his most significant battle-zone move being the reinstatement of von Rundstedt, in the role of Commander-in-Chief West, with the remit to stabilise and reinforce the West Wall.

Whether or not von Rundstedt's efforts could have enabled the offensive to have been mounted earlier, there was still the mighty logistical nightmare of getting the force together for the task. It is clear that Hitler wanted to get the initiative in hand in early November but von Rundstedt could not report the West Wall secure until late October so delay was inevitable. Although all new military production had been set aside for his still secret plan for some weeks and a few troops were being brought back from the Balkans and elsewhere, he was setting so much store in his counter-strike that even his bravado had been kept in check by regular doses of realism. He had been aware from his first thoughts of such an offensive that an essential element of its success would be surprise.

Only after his dramatic outburst could his plans be more widely implemented, though von Rundstedt and Model were still not included in this small privi-

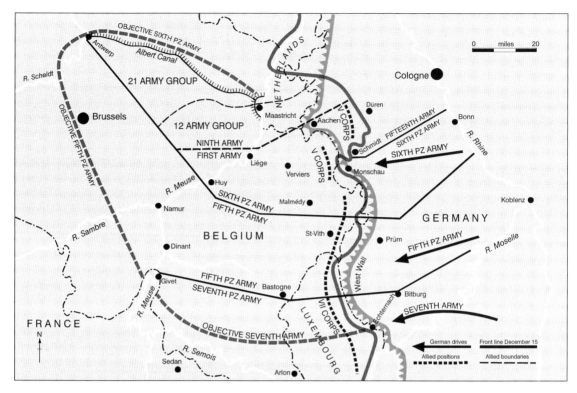

THE GERMAN PLAN

leged group. The next three weeks saw an explosion of activity in which Jodl was now charged with putting some 'flesh on the bones' of his leader's skeletal scheme, to make it an operational plan rather than an ill-considered pipe-dream. At this point the principal requirements of the final plan were: start date between 20 and 30 November; route through the Ardennes; beachheads over the Meuse between Liège and Namur, securing of Antwerp and its port; British and Canadian forces kept north of a line Antwerp–Liège/Bastogne, and engaged there; deployment of 30 divisions including 10 armoured divisions; availability of major artillery and rocket projector units; major Luftwaffe participation; full use of tactical surprise and speed; strictly limited number of personnel preparing the plan; maintenance of absolute security.

Jodl was much more than a 'military secretary'; an intimate confidant, his ability to transpose the terse and ignorant pronouncements of his leader into logical and intelligent orders was a major asset that kept him close to Hitler. By the time he returned with a considered plan, he had worked through five options and selected two to put forward. The first saw a single thrust through the Venlo area towards Antwerp, the second featured a dual routing through northern Luxembourg and north-west of Aachen that would meet up before the drive on to the main objective. Hitler told Jodl he wanted the second option but the detailed plan presented on 11 October saw the Führer's favoured Ardennes route given the greater emphasis and from this point the detailed planning went into overdrive.

It was, of course, remarkable that neither von Rundstedt nor Model yet knew of this major offensive operation, but even more astonishing was the fact that it was their chiefs of staff who were first, beyond Hitler's immediate staff, to hear of it. General Westphal, from von Rundstedt's team, and General Krebs, chief of Model's Army Group B staff, were called to Hitler's headquarters in East Prussia on 22 October and will surely have arrived in sombre mood, fearing a tirade; the news from the front continued to be bad, with Aachen having just fallen to the Allies and Hitler undoubtedly angered by their constant calls for more men and equipment to protect the route to the Ruhr. In the event, after being sworn to secrecy on pain of death, they were not asked for reports but given one; an operation called 'Wacht am Rhein' (Watch on the Rhine) was to be mounted and they *were* to get men and weapons, though for offensive rather than defensive action.

By now the whole event was liable to be delayed, but Hitler's personal briefing to Westphal and Krebs was still thoroughly upbeat and nominated 20 November for the completion of the build-up and 25 November for the first offensive moves. The two generals would be allocated eighteen infantry and twelve armoured divisions and these would include paratroop divisions and panzer units. The Luftwaffe would support the operation and more than enough fuel supplies were being found. Whether Hitler told the generals that the dates for attack had been taken after advice from his meteorologists is not clear, but it can be assumed that they were more concerned that the promised reinforcements would actually arrive this time. Their other priority now was a swift return to their respective field marshals to report on the dramatic news they had just received.

Field Marshal von Rundstedt had seen most things in war, had been asked to perform military miracles on more that one occasion, and surely deserved better treatment than he was being given here. Certainly he had the respect of Hitler, Jodl and Keitel, but for his military experience and dogged attention to detail, not for his support for the cause of National Socialism for he was transparently non-political and was Prussian first and foremost. Having been retired because of Hitler's displeasure at perceived battlefield failure, he had now been called back because the Führer needed him, but that didn't gain him access to the inner circle and he was tolerated for the standing he brought to his post rather than any overt loyalty or genuine endorsement of the cause. On receiving Westphal's report, this grand old man of the German Army would have had mixed reactions, mostly negative. His pride would have been hurt because of his lack of involvement in the planning and the derogatory way in which the news was transmitted to him. He would have felt early anguish that this ill-considered plan would result in the loss of more good German men and prejudice his country's future, but he would have admired elements of the plan – 'the operational idea as it stands could be considered a stroke of genius' – and took some encouragement from the thought of the Army being deployed offensively.

Model was a different animal. He had played up to Hitler more markedly, was an enthusiast for the Nazi cause, and demonstrably more ambitious for himself than was his older colleague. The two men were, however, respectful of each other even if not great friends and were somewhat united by the news Westphal and Krebs brought them for, while both may have had a surge of enthusiasm at the promise of more men and equipment and the chance to see a military counter to the Allied advance, neither was convinced that the strategy was sound and workable. As a result, both worked feverishly on alternative schemes.

The older man could only recognise the advantage of surprise and the gamble of using the Ardennes where the opposition was at its weakest; elsewhere he felt the ultimate goal of Antwerp was unattainable with the forces being allocated to the task. He was unconvinced that the promised reinforcements would materialise – he had been let down before. He felt that the Allies might themselves recommence the offensive before the German plan could be activated, and he believed that the logistical support for a very rapid advance could not be maintained, that forces he had wanted for defence of the nation could be lost in salients cut off by Allied ripostes. He proposed an alternative whose immediate aim was to destroy opposition forces rather than regain Antwerp; in principle, a tighter breakthrough on a narrower front than Hitler proposed. Its attraction was that it could still cause the Allied forces to halt, even withdraw, and would at least give them a 'bloody nose'; perhaps von Rundstedt believed the propaganda from his leader that the Americans in particular would be found to have no stomach for the fight once they had tasted something other than outright success. It was a cautious plan, matching the character of its creator, and it would not appeal to Hitler as it did not offer the early prize of Antwerp and its port.

Model had quickly dismissed the plan as relayed to him by Krebs; he felt that it didn't 'have a damned leg to stand on', and felt too that Antwerp was a hopeless goal. Model's revisions brought armoured thrusts into the piece much earlier than Rundstedt's and dismissed the sense of a two-pronged attack. The Army Group B formula worked on a forward drive along a 40-mile front with two Panzer armies in the vanguard.

Just two weeks after their first sight of 'Wacht am Rhein', the two field marshals met to compare notes, but total agreement was never likely and only the futility of keeping Antwerp as the ultimate goal saw them in accord. A combined effort was put forward to High Command, taking in most of von Rundstedt's thinking, but it mattered little for when Jodl presented it to Hitler he quickly condemned it as small-minded and unadventurous … he would not be moved. Von Rundstedt received his leader's final instructions shortly after they were signed on 1 November; he would give grudging support to what he considered a foolish exercise and Model would have to do his best to implement it. No one had persuaded the Führer substantially to modify his base plan; Antwerp was still the goal, the dictate was unalterable.

It should be remembered that it was not just Model and von Rundstedt who opposed the plan. Dietrich and von Manteuffel, both destined to play a major role, were also sceptical, which is especially interesting if one considers the long-term allegiance of the former. Von Rundstedt did respond again, insisting that the men and equipment allocated were still insufficient even to hold ground taken, let alone drive on to Antwerp, but it was a gesture intended to place his disenchantment on record rather than expected to induce a last-minute change of mind. This did not stop the two field marshals from continuing to promote a more modest plan, but in truth von Rundstedt's involvement from this point changed from minimal to nil and, despite the Allies' belief to the contrary, he took no part in overseeing the action save for a final communiqué to the troops at the start of the Offensive.

Throughout all this planning, bad news continued to arrive from all fronts and divisions earmarked for 'Wacht' had to be re-directed to or retained at points where opposition forces were pressing, east of Aachen and around Metz. This did not deter the German leader who had again to remind the field marshals that he was not for turning when he sent Jodl to meet them on 26 November, and this position was strengthened when von Manteuffel and Dietrich were eventually persuaded by Model to back the alternative plan at a meeting called by Hitler in Berlin on 2 December. It was now well-known that the Führer was promising a staggering four and a quarter million gallons of extra engine fuel and fifty train loads of extra ammunition. A final battle plan put forward by the field marshals a few days later was again rejected and the operation order to proceed with his plan was issued by Hitler on 9 December. The much delayed Ardennes Offensive would begin soon. While the generals had feverishly maintained that it would have to be abandoned if the Allies began a major advance first, this threat never materialised; there were few significant moves made by Eisenhower in the first weeks of November. Just two divisions set aside for 'Wacht am Rhein' were called into action elsewhere with Army Group G.

Indeed, at this point, the Allied High Command was still planning rather than fighting; the few battlefield initiatives were not distracting Eisenhower's determination to get his next moves right. In a meeting with Field Marshal Montgomery, Air Chief Marshal Tedder and General Bradley in Maastricht on 7 December it was agreed that a major offensive should begin early in the New Year, though the exact nature of this action was not so easily decided upon; Montgomery was pressing for a main attack north of the Ruhr with 21 Army Group while Eisenhower had always favoured a second thrust by Patton's Third Army, towards Frankfurt. In the following days the principal Allied action would be clearing up various 'loose ends' and pockets of obstructing German forces so that the main drive, probably in the second week of 1945, could commence from a 'clean' setting-off point. There was no great consideration of the forces in the sector of the front the German leader had been studying; it remained the 'quiet zone'. The Allies would be by-passing the Ardennes when they attacked for they

Above: The Ardennes area abounded in tree-lined roads that were easy to defend.

considered it virtually impassable and certainly unsuitable for any form of swift advance.

The troops of US First Army were manning the front from Aachen to just south of Luxembourg and, of these, Major General Troy Middleton's VIII Corps, on the right flank, were among the most relaxed. Two of his infantry division were resting after the November advance to the Roer and a third had just arrived from the USA. Their remit was to rest, train and observe the enemy, a blessed relief after the casualty-ridden fighting of the previous months.

Thus it was that when, on 11 and 12 December, Hitler finally outlined his until now private plan for the Ardennes to his generals he must have felt that he had chosen his tactics wisely. There had been no major Allied initiative of the type von Rundstedt and Model feared, and the Allied aircraft, if not entirely halted by the onset of the full German winter, were having to reduce their missions by the day as mists precluded worthwhile activity. In a long, wide-ranging sermon that must have physically drained him, he stressed several points: perseverance, strength of purpose, the value of attack as opposed to purely defensive tactics, the feuding in the Allied command, and the incompatibility of the Allied grouping where each faction had a different agenda. He avoided detail, for the 'devil' was certainly there on this occasion; the lack of fuel despite the extras promised, absence of worthwhile air support, shortage of experienced troops … it would have been a litany of reasons *not* to mount the counter-offensive he was presenting. So, just as he had always used his self-assurance to transmit the battle cry, now, though certainly aware of the minimal chance of success, he used grand phrases and evangelical rhetoric rather than the detail of strategic particulars, though he did make reference to the advantages the German tanks still enjoyed over the British and American vehicles, and regularly reminded his audience of the loss of life already inflicted on the Allied armies.

Not surprisingly, no mention was made of the fact that Germany was almost without allies at this point; even the Japanese were urging Hitler to begin negotiations with the Soviets, and erstwhile partners were turning away from the Nazi cause and changing sides.

If not the ideal fighting ground, the Ardennes certainly was the weakest link in the chain of Allied forces; it would have been tempting for the most cautious military commander, but for one who had seen his forces sweep through the region in their prime, just a few short years before, it was overwhelmingly attractive. At this time the Allied front line stretched across 500 miles, but was at its strongest north of the Ardennes, where the forces were gathered for the vital fight for the Ruhr industrial area, and to the south, for the run to the Saar. As we have established, just five divisions defended the 80 miles of the Allied front across the Ardennes and most of these were made up of newly arrived or recuperating units. Hitler's troops knew the area better than their opponents, would be more confident operating within it, and both sides knew that the winter months would bring mists and snow; one could nullify the Allied air supremacy, the other might bring out the best in the German infantry.

It should be remembered here that the one-time vivid orator capable of spellbinding, euphoria-inducing speeches was now a bent, shuffling, pallid and unsteady man to whom these afflictions had come suddenly and early – he was 54 years of age; his appearance could not portray the vibrancy and enthusiasm needed on this occasion. He was lame, heavily medicated, subject to memory loss that was not deliberate and physically weak through months of incarceration that prevented exercise or even adequate fresh air. His will was undimmed and he still craved victory in one form or another, but here, lecturing the men who would participate in his last military gamble, he had to depend for their attention on heavy, threatening security that forbade dispute or dissent.

Those attending the Führer's presentation – more a rabid lecture – were bussed to the 'Adlershorst' (Eagle's Nest) near Bad Nauheim and stripped of document cases, side-arms and other personal belongings before moving down to the bunker where security remained oppressive with more SS personnel than visitors; it must have been a forbidding atmosphere even for these hardened men of war. None of the generals had the updated knowledge of the entire war situation the Führer enjoyed and thus, even if they doubted his upbeat message or could summon up the bravado to question his remarks, they were not in a position to use facts in support of their case.

However unconvinced they were that they could repeat the 'Blitzkrieg' techniques used in the drive through the Ardennes in 1940, some must have warmed to the challenge of a return to the successful tactics of the past. Others, of course, were well aware that the shortage of troops and weapons was not a figment of their imagination and therefore this crazy scheme was a dream not worthy of the same military minds that had swept their army through to France. Short of the arrival of the planned new devastating weaponry Hitler kept promising, the only chance the German forces had of striking back at the Allies, and delaying their advance, *was* the implementation of the 'Blitzkreig' mentality, of using the core elements of that technique, but could he muster these basic components together?

He assured the gathering that the Luftwaffe was set to give all the necessary air support, that there were sufficient tanks and munitions for the job, and that there were hundreds of thousands of troops available. In truth, the Luftwaffe would have far too few aircraft and mostly outdated ones at that; there would certainly not be enough ammunition for the tanks and artillery, and the troops were to be made up in good part of reservists – either very old or too young and inexperienced. Hitler was able, however, to boast one of the major tenets of the 'Blitzkrieg' philosophy … the element of surprise.

No one, not the enemy or even his principal military advisers, thought Hitler's Germany currently capable of mounting a significant counter-offensive. Certainly the Allies were aware that their onward progress would be met by stiff defence, but surely not counter-attack?

The Führer knew that he was incapable of an attack across a truly broad front, but if he used what forces he could muster and set them on a relatively narrow course where the Allies were most thinly spread, he might achieve the necessary concentration of action and, given successful implementation to that point, might even achieve the third requirement of the strategy – speed. Surprise, concentration and speed, the recipe for 'Blitzkrieg'; could the first create the second and third? He first had to convince the generals that they could undertake the challenge and then make sure that they tackled it with commitment and efficiency.

The momentum of 'Blitzkrieg' was not easy to achieve from a standing start, let alone one that found the participants already on the back foot. In the drives to the west and east earlier in the war, the strategy had been employed almost without pause – it was only checked once it stopped of its own accord or was forced to by pervasive opposition. For the Ardennes in 1944 he had to secure ground, break the enemy and move on with the same awesome pace and destructive power of those years before; would this be possible again?

Gerd von Rundstedt admired the bravado shown by choosing the Ardennes since, for all of his formal and traditional strategic thinking, he still understood the reasoning, especially the value of surprise. But the veteran did not share his leader's optimism about the eventual outcome; he felt that failure was certain and his apathy ensured that his role in the effort would be nominal, the commander in name only so as to encourage the efforts of the men in the ranks. Model, who was to be the commander in the field, was equally pessimistic.

ARMIES AND LEADERS
THE ALLIED FORCES

Eisenhower could call upon 65 divisions in three major commands: Bradley's 12 Army Group had twenty-nine, Montgomery's 21 Army Group nineteen and Jacob Devers' 6 Army Group seventeen.

Dwight David Eisenhower

Below: Photographic evidence. Eisenhower betrays silent torture as Montgomery makes a point with a typically pompous pose. The American Supreme Commander showed fine judgement and extreme patience in his work with the Englishman.

When America entered the war and posted forces to the European and Pacific theatres. it brought with it some military commanders of outstanding merit; the most notable was Eisenhower. If he was a 'director of operations' rather than a battlefield general this was no loss to the Allied cause for, if anything, it was his ability to manage people and plans through the complexities of a major war that distinguished him and enabled him to perform his difficult task so well.

Although he had not fought in the First World War, he had spent those years raising the first US tank corps and ultimately commanded 10,000 men. His performance in that role, and his work on the staffs of 1914–18 veteran General Pershing and of Douglas MacArthur, set this young man on a meteoric rise to senior posts which saw him appointed Commanding General of the European Theatre of Operations in London when the North Africa Campaign was being planned; as Pershing was the natural choice to lead the AEF in Europe in 1917,

so Eisenhower was the prime candidate for this new Allied role, even though he had never experienced 'live war'. Eisenhower had not supported the 'Torch' landings when the feasibility was being discussed in Washington – he was for opening a second front in Europe – but, once there, he employed typical resolution, conciliation and judgement in pressing forward the Allied endeavour.

In his position as Supreme Commander of the Allied Expeditionary Forces for Operation 'Overlord' he used his expertise in tough diplomacy to ensure that the mixed forces, and especially the joint commands, worked in unison. Once the Allied forces had broken out of Normandy, he insisted that the retreating enemy be pursued along a broad front. His insistence on this when others, such as Montgomery and Patton, were either pressing for narrower thrusts or actually moving almost too fast for the overall tactic to work, looked to have been ill-founded when the sudden counter by Hitler through the Ardennes caused short-term chaos. Eisenhower himself was certainly surprised by the German move – like his commanders and his Intelligence teams, he thought the opposition to be incapable of such a strike – but his speed of reaction and prompt decision-making were enough to foil the attack. Although his senior officers were surprised by his assertion that the Ardennes thrust by Model represented an 'opportunity for us and not a disaster', he was proved to be right ... not for the first time. The Battle of the Bulge certainly proved to be an opportunity for Eisenhower .... to demonstrate his man-management and executive skill once more.

Bernard Montgomery

An undistinguished performance at Sandhurst quickly put behind him, Bernard Montgomery saw action as a platoon commander in the First World War – he was badly wounded in the head – and then performed well in various staff positions before reaching the rank of lieutenant-colonel and battalion commander. In 1940 he was commanding 3rd Division in the British Expeditionary Force, and was evacuated with his men from Dunkirk.

The death of General William Gort, Churchill's first choice to succeed Auchinleck as commander of Eighth Army in Africa, saw Montgomery chosen in his place. Benefiting from the fresh supply of men and equipment Churchill had earmarked for Gort, the new man set about improving British fortunes in the region and was able to secure the first substantial victory of the war at El Alamein, though the achievement was somewhat tarnished by his preference for the cautionary approach. This desert action saw him become a national hero overnight, and he relished his new status.

After initiating the action in Sicily and the Italian mainland, Montgomery was called home to take part in the planning for D-Day. Now that the European theatre had become an Allied operation, Montgomery found himself reporting to Eisenhower with consequent clashes of opinion on strategy. Perhaps only Eisenhower could have kept 'Monty' truly focused at this time, though Harold Alexander had established something of a blueprint solution for this potential problem in North Africa.

Once the invasion was under way, Montgomery enjoyed the relative freedom of the battlefield again and was successful in driving the Germans back. Although there were times when he moved too slowly for some of his American colleagues, Montgomery was satisfying Eisenhower, save for his constant call for a narrower front. When Eisenhower agreed to Montgomery's plan to cross the Rhine at Arnhem he was sanctioning a risk-laden scheme that turned into a débâcle, though the end result was a somewhat more acquiescent British colleague!

When 21 Army Group, with Montgomery in command, was called upon to help repulse the German rush into the Ardennes he approached the challenge with full resolve and enthusiasm and the eventual victory enabled the Allied crossing of the Rhine just south of where he had failed at Arnhem a few months before. But he was as surprised by the German initiative as anyone, reporting on 16 December that, 'the enemy is at present fighting a defensive campaign on all fronts; his situation is such that he cannot stage major offensive operations … nor could his tanks compete with ours in a mobile battle.[3]

'Monty's' demeanour was sufficient to offend many of the Americans with whom he was working; his officious, egotistical nature and penchant for self-promotion did not fit well with the more liberal style of his Allied colleagues and it seemed to them to be out of place on the battlefield. But he was dedicated to his task and hugely supportive of his men, this showing itself in his regular pleas for more men and *matériel*. He was too cautious at times and occasionally failed to see the broader picture, but for all his faults he got the job done more effectively than most.

Right: A firm handshake, but Omar Bradley did not welcome sharing command with Montgomery when it was imposed on him by Eisenhower.

Omar N. Bradley

It is a further testament to Eisenhower's man-management skill that in his role of Supreme Allied Commander he was working with contemporaries to whom he had to give leadership, and both credit and admonishment. Bradley was a West Point classroom colleague of Eisenhower's and, like him, had not seen battlefield service in 1917. His career also bore a symmetry with Patton's, from whom he took over in North Africa, and to whom he was both a subordinate and a superior at various times.

The two worked well in North Africa, with Bradley enjoying a special success when he stormed Bizerta and took 40,000 prisoners. He was keenly aware that his infantry skills could complement Eisenhower's tactical astuteness; the same co-ordination was effective during 'Overlord' and the drive on Paris. Bradley sided with Eisenhower in the debate about the method of counter-attacking the Germans, leaving Montgomery isolated, but this unity was disrupted when the Supreme Commander assigned the US First Army to Montgomery rather than Bradley after the American had been found to be so unprepared for the Ardennes Offensive. This setback was an affront to so loyal a partner, but his battlefield acumen was not undermined and his sharp thinking enabled Bastogne to be held and Patton launched on a flanking move to relieve it.

To Eisenhower, Omar Bradley was a trusted field commander who could be relied upon to employ a given strategy with coolness and thoroughness. His unassuming, undemonstrative air hid a steely determination; he was never daunted by having large forces under his command and his attention to detail was legendary.

Below: George Patton shows the cheery and confident persona for which he was known. He had a great rapport with his men despite driving them hard.

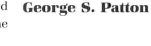

George S. Patton

Patton and Montgomery had few things in common. Perhaps both relished military glory and were able to get the best from their troops but, where the Englishman was formal, traditional and conservative on and off the battlefield, Patton was unconventional, flamboyant and entirely free from airs and graces. There would have been some friction between them wherever they might have met.

'Blood and Guts' Patton was a tank man. He marvelled at the invention and each advance in its technology, and was a fervent believer in its effectiveness. He had served in a US tank corps in 1917–18, and he arrived at the 'Torch' landings, and subsequent European events, certain that this was the weapon to bring Allied victory. He had considerable personal drive and expected the same from his officers and men, sometimes to the point of plainly unfair treatment and unjust requests; he was once demoted after reportedly slapping the face of a soldier he came across in a military hospital suffering from 'combat fatigue'.

After the Normandy landings the pace at which he drove his men forward was both remarkable and, at times, unwise; time and

again it was necessary to halt so that adjacent forces could catch up or his supply lines be modified. At the Battle of the Bulge his intervention was clinical and
decisive, with rapid changes of direction enabling his troops to help relieve
Bastogne and accelerate the thrust towards the Rhine.

Tough and resourceful, toting two ivory-handled pistols reputedly taken from
Pancho Villa during Pershing's 1916 raid into Mexico, and capable of the crudest
language, Patton was an 'all-American' character who was also a widely read,
religious and caring man.

Jacob L. Devers   After taking command of the Allied forces for Operation 'Dragoon', the landing in southern France, Devers took just three weeks to secure the planned
link with the 'Overlord' troops advancing across the north. He drove forward to
and beyond Strasbourg where he was required to hold his line just short of the
German border during the Ardennes offensive. Once the Allied advance was
under way again, Devers led his forces to take Munich and Berchtesgaden.

Courtney Hicks Hodges   To have been appointed Omar Bradley's deputy in US First Army
was a decent achievement for someone who had failed his exam-
inations at West Point and entered military service as a private. He was commissioned in 1909 and decorated on two occasions during the First World War.

Early in the 1939–45 period Hodges was Chief of Intelligence, but was given
the leadership of X Corps at the end of 1942. He was promoted to Lieutenant
General of Third Army in 1943, but moved again when Bradley's 12 Army Group
was formed, assuming command of First Army, which he led into some of the
most demanding battles. Prior to the Ardennes he captured Aachen and then
took the bridge at Remagen before meeting up with the Red Army near Torgau.
He later served in the Pacific and participated at Okinawa.

Hodges was a bluff, private man who 'got on with the job' and cared little for
the inner political manoeuvring that invariably accompanied a major conflict.
His great expertise in infantry warfare contributed hugely to the final Allied push
to the Rhine and beyond.

Leonard T. Gerow   Gerow was another example of the bluff, tough and uncompromising battlefield commander who served the Allied forces so well in the drive from
Normandy. He had been at the General Staff College with Eisenhower, had
served in the Philippines and fought the Japanese in Shanghai. As commander
of V Corps he brought his men from Normandy to the Ardennes in a constant
state of battle readiness, using his resources in a judicious rotational scheme
that kept up the momentum of the advance.

Robert W. Hasbrouck   He was in command of US 7th Armored Division when it was hurried to St-Vith to strengthen the defences of that strategic town. He
had his men cover the 90 miles from Aachen, on the Dutch border, in twelve

hours and pitched them straight into battle without delay. His calm and resourcefulness in the defensive action he was required to undertake in appalling conditions earned extreme admiration and severely dented the German advance in this important sector.

Anthony McAuliffe

McAuliffe was divisional commander of 101st Airborne Division at the time of the greatest threat to those surrounded at Bastogne when von Lüttwitz allowed a delegation to the American forces proposing their surrender. This bluff, no nonsense 46-year-old is said to have responded, 'Aw, nuts' and, at the suggestion of his staff, allowed that to be his official reply.

Left: General
Anthony McAuliffe.

THE GERMAN FORCES

Hitler allocated 64 divisions to the West Front during his Ardennes operation. Army Group G made up the southern sector and had twenty-one divisions under General Hermann Balck, Army Group B was under the command of Model and boasted twenty-five, and Army Group H, in the north under Kurt Student, had eleven; the remainder were to be held in reserve.

Gerd von Rundstedt

When Adolf Hitler was seeking to delay or stop the Allied advance across the Rhine, von Rundstedt was already sixty-nine years old and had 'retired' or sought to retire on numerous occasions. A graduate of the renowned *Kriegsakademie* and active throughout 1914–18, von Rundstedt was a Lieutenant-General when Hitler came to power and could already claim a distinguished service record of loyalty and achievement. He was not, however, enamoured of the new leader who, to so regimented a man, seemed unconventional and intransigent. Once the war had started, Hitler needed von Rundstedt more than the veteran needed him; the Führer believed that with this man of Prussian military background alongside him the support of the officer corps was more likely, though he found the older man rigid, theoretical and dour. Their relationship was tense; each disliked the other, but Hitler realised that the older man was liked and respected by the public and admired by the troops.

The ageing General was keen to retire after surviving the 1938 purge, but was instead put in command of Second Army during the Sudetenland drama. Even when retirement was allowed it was short-lived; he was brought back to plan the Polish campaign and then command HQ Army Group South and Army Group A. The veteran must have taken pride in the success of the German drive into France, though he did not distinguish himself when holding his tanks back from the low ground around Dunkirk in the belief that the Luftwaffe could attack the retreating British Expeditionary Force. He was far from enthusiastic about the idea of invading England, although he was put in charge of the planning for the aborted operation.

During his time on the Eastern Front he suffered a heart-attack and again retired, but was back in command for the occupation of Vichy France and in confronting the Allied invasion in 1944.

Von Rundstedt was respected by Allied commanders. The acute tactical mind of this experienced military professional and Prussian aristocrat was well-known to them and they held the unfounded belief that the Ardennes battle plan was his work. In fact he had little input and it was Hitler himself and his inner circle at the time who conceived it. Even so, he appears to have admired its audacity, but believed it unachievable, and, though he was nominally in charge, was kept well in the background and without the power to influence events.

Walther Model

Born Otto Moritz Walther Model on 24 January 1891 in Genthin in the Prussian province of Brandenburg, the man who was to become one of Hitler's most loyal generals grew up among a family of choral musicians in surroundings of art and culture. He was a sickly child but was drawn to the colourful, regimental life of the military and pursued that career against the odds of one whose physical condition and mental courage did not mark him as a potential battlefield leader.

In 1914 he was adjutant of 1st Battalion, 52nd Infantry Regiment. Despite promotion he remained with his men in the trenches and was shot in the neck in May 1915. Later, on the recommendation of Prince Oskar of Prussia, he was sent on a General Staff Course, which he passed with honours and so gained further promotions. Rather than be allowed to drift back into civilian life at the end of the war, Model was retained within the Army structure and given opportunities to plan for whatever military future the Treaty of Versailles would allow Germany. He learned to evade the strictures of that agreement and was responsible for recruiting and organising paramilitary units which, though abandoned by the Nazis when they came to power, kept alive the military spirit which otherwise might have evaporated.

By October 1935 Hitler had noted Model's worth and placed him in charge of Section 8 of the Army General Staff with the rank of major-general, a role that saw him visit Spain during the Civil War to evaluate the performance and weaponry of each side. The outbreak of war in 1939 saw Model held back from the battlefield until made Chief of Staff of Sixteenth Army on the Western Front and then transferred East for Operation 'Barbarossa'. In the German advance Model, like his senior colleagues, was an efficient leader but when the fortunes turned he was almost alone in retaining belief in the Führer and his cause. His defensive fighting strategies often went unpunished by Berlin because they were clearly well planned and considered; indeed he was one of few of his time that were as capable in defence as in attack. He even persuaded his leader of the merits of delaying action around Kursk until reinforcements arrived. To defend his acquiescence to such moves, the Führer would often declare Model's plans to be part of schemes for later counter-attack. It was no accident that Model became known as 'Hitler's Fireman' for, where others would query instructions or show a lack of resolve, this man of hard-working, ethical Prussian stock, could be sent into any situation with the certainty that he would act loyally and resourcefully. His decisions were always well considered and therefore not easy to argue against; he was a fine tactician, a devoted planner and a studious director of troops.

Benefiting from this special relationship with his leader while others were becoming disillusioned, Model – whom Hitler described as 'my best field marshal' – was a logical choice to lead the Ardennes counter-offensive. He believed Hitler's assurances that it was crucial to delay the Allied advance until the 'new weaponry' arrived. That the plan failed was not Model's fault, but when he and his 325,000 men were trapped in the Ruhr in April 1945 he realised there was no way that even he could deliver the result Hitler required. After spending some days with some of his officers in the countryside east of Düsseldorf, apparently contemplating the fate of his country, he walked alone into a nearby wood and,

Above: Walther Model commanded Hitler's operation on the ground but was openly sceptical of its chances for success.

on 21 April, committed suicide by shooting himself, and, by doing so, set his Führer an example to the last. This devout Christian, husband and father, was unable to accept the humiliation of capture or of failing the German people.

Josef ('Sepp') Dietrich

This native of Hawangen in Swabia reached military command by a vastly different route from von Rundstedt and Model. Although he had fought during the First World War, enlisting in the 7th Field Artillery of the Bavarian Army in August 1914 just two days after Great Britain's declaration of war and seeing action in Flanders a few weeks later, he was not of well-educated military stock nor did his battlefield experience give him a profession in the inter-war years. In that period he held a range of menial jobs – including that of a butcher's assistant – until his enthusiastic work for the National Socialist Workers' Association brought him to the attention of the young Adolf Hitler who, never failing to make use of a like-minded character eager for work, promptly gave him various modest jobs within his close network.

When the Nazis came to power Hitler was able to move Dietrich through the ranks of the Party at a greater pace than his intellect or performance merited. Now with rank he had always craved, Dietrich recognised this patronage and rewarded it with unstinting loyalty and a readiness to carry out the most heinous acts in the cause of protecting his master and furthering the cause.

Right: As the hapless go-between, Alfred Jodl had to implement Hitler's plan as best he could with his concessions to the advice of Model and von Rundstedt kept to a minimum.

Far right: His acquiescence with Hitler's most crazed demands ensured Wilhelm Keitel's position close to the Führer. He was a loyal sycophant to the end.

Not that Hitler was unsure of what Dietrich could offer – he referred to him as 'simultaneously cunning, energetic and brutal', while von Rundstedt classed him as 'decent but stupid'. Indeed, it is a remarkable commentary on the military hierarchy under Hitler that two 'vons' – Rundstedt and Manteuffel – had to share a similar status with this common, less talented man. However accurate the above descriptions may be, we must not rely on Dietrich's own account of his military career for it is littered with inaccuracies and false claims.

Although he showed bravery in the attack on Paris and on the Eastern Front, Dietrich could claim only a fraction of the 'live war' experience of his fellow officers involved in the Ardennes counter-offensive, but his work when in command of Hitler's special bodyguard (the Waffen SS) had proved his commitment to independent action and a callous disregard for the principles of warfare, the very qualities Hitler felt he wanted to be shown by Sixth SS Panzer Army. Certainly he relished the difficulties of operating in the snow-covered forests of the Ardennes where unconventional modes of warfare would be effective. He had great confidence in small unit actions, but his inability to cope with large-scale operations was soon evident and he made little impact.

Dietrich survived the defeat, and the war, though his regard for his Führer disappeared when, in April 1945 on the Russian Front, his officers and men were ordered by Hitler to be stripped of their armbands in punishment for poor performance. At a post-war tribunal Dietrich was sentenced to 25 years' imprisonment for the murder of 71 American prisoners at Malmédy during the Battle of the Bulge. He was released after ten years and, after serving another shorter prison sentence, died in 1966.

Freiherr Hasso von Manteuffel

Following strong performances on the Eastern Front, he was placed in charge of Fifth Panzer Army after the Ardennes plan was already in hand, with the remit to push on to Brussels once the breakthrough had been achieved. Like his fellow officers, he was handicapped by lack of air support, ammunition, fuel and provisions, and his desperate requests to Berlin for these went unheeded as the Allies struck back.

He was a very small man, thin, almost haggard, but this belied a steely disposition which showed itself in decisiveness and an ability to assess his situation and react effectively; wherever possible he would get up to the front line and show that he was willing to share the same dangers as his men. He later commanded Third Panzer Army in another lost cause in the east; after the war, he entered politics.

Alfred Jodl

Chief of the Operations Staff and Hitler's right-hand man. He, Keitel and Warlimont, formed the subservient trio who implemented Hitler's military dictates. He was asked to assess the needs and processes that would make the Ardennes action a success and did so as best he could considering the unrealistic expectations of his leader. He was ambitious for the seniority he came to enjoy, but was completely deferential in his relationship with Hitler. He signed the German surrender at Reims on 7 May 1945. He was hanged at Nuremberg.

Wilhelm Keitel   Known to those who did not appreciate his unquestioning loyalty to Hitler as 'Yes-Keitel' and 'the nodding ass', this veteran of 1914–18 was one of the Führer's inner circle for the duration of the war. This did not bring power and influence but simply the satisfaction of status in return for doing his master's bidding in all things. He did much of the ground work for the Ardennes offensive but was simply implementing the edicts of Hitler in doing so. He was hanged at Nuremberg.

Fritz Bayerlein   He commanded the Panzer Lehr Division with a tough and uncompromising attitude which brought out some fine performances in the Normandy Campaign, and was fighting American units along the Saar when called upon for the Ardennes action after a minor refit; here he was not so effective and certainly was inactive for too long in the Bastogne area. His colourful reports of Hitler's briefing of the generals just before the offensive was launched told of a heavy SS presence that made delegates wary of making even the slightest move, let alone speaking against the plan.

Freiherr Friedrich-August von der Heydte   A paratroop veteran of the doom-laden airborne assault on Crete, he was prevented from using his own forces during the Ardennes action because of the intelligence risk in bringing them to the front. Instead he was given 800 men of doubtful pedigree drawn from the various forward regiments of II *Fallschirmkorps*, a motley group that inevitably failed to achieve their objective. Their transport aircraft were poorly piloted – only a fraction of the men were dropped on target, and their objective was reduced to reconnaissance work.

Hermann Balck   A veteran of 1914–18, Balck was a soldier's soldier. Conscious of the well-being and concerns of his men, he was a fine motivator and a prime exponent of tactical advance, so a natural choice for involvement in the Ardennes.

A soldier first and a Nazi second, he was often criticised by the Führer for failing to halt the Allied advance, but one suspects that his attributes were readily recognised by Hitler, who continued to employ him from the outset of the war until the end.

Kurt Student   A pilot during the First World War, he was an early recruit to the nascent Luftwaffe and was chosen by Göring to mastermind the development of paratroops. He proved an innovative strategist whose airborne forces played a significant role in the years of 'Blitzkrieg' and, while his well-executed assault on

Crete proved too costly in terms of lives and caused Hitler to forbid any further actions on that scale, he remained at the forefront of paratroops and their deployment.

Heinrich von Lüttwitz

This small, stout and monocled man began his military life in the lower ranks, volunteering for service at the outset of World War One. This slow start did not hold him back for, within a year, he was commissioned, became a cavalry officer and, as the new weapon became more common on the battlefield, an expert in tanks and armoured strategy. Spoken of as a 'passionate soldier' and much loved by the men he led, he was tolerant of the limitations of his troops. His appearance belied an energetic man whose performance around Bastogne blighted an otherwise effective career.

Erich Brandenberger

A formal and reserved man whose dour and stolid adherence to orders left little room for the initiative required of a field commander. This incurred the displeasure of Model on more than one occasion, but he had proved himself on the Eastern Front where determination and rigidity counted for more than invention and innovative thinking.

Jochen Peiper

It was Peiper who, commanding a Waffen SS Combat group, got closer to the Führer's first target of the River Meuse than any other unit. Though his progress showed what might have been achieved had other groups shown his determination and drive, his advance was reckless and ill-considered for it failed to take account of other parts of his force and the need to ensure adequate logistical support. He was, as a result, left isolated and without results to show for his efforts. He will forever be associated with the Malmédy massacre on 17th December for which, along with other atrocities, he was sentenced to death, though later reprieved.

Otto Skorzeny

This military adventurer was Germany's foremost special forces man; the organiser of many of the early deployments of special purpose units, he was highly regarded by Hitler who saw in these tactics an additional 'new weapon'. Skorzeny became known by the Allies as 'the most dangerous man in Europe' after his rescue of Mussolini and the kidnapping of the Hungarian leader's son, but for the Ardennes Offensive he was to mount Operation 'Greif' (Griffin) using a mixed collection of English-speaking SS commandos, paratroops and others, including some air and tank crew personnel. His men were to dress as Americans, drive American jeeps and infiltrate Allied forces in order to capture and secure bridges over the Meuse before the Americans, whom Hitler expected to be retreating over that natural barrier, could demolish them. In the event, while the units did cause some confusion and unease, they never achieved their aim because of the slow progress of the German advance.

4
WEAPONS
AMERICAN WEAPONS AND EQUIPMENT

The ubiquitous M4 Sherman tank was the most common armoured vehicle in the Allied forces in their advance across northern Europe, and in the Ardennes. Nevertheless, the German PzKpfw IVs and Panthers were superior.

From the very first action after D-Day, the Sherman's firepower was seen to be inferior to the enemy's vehicles: the 75mm M3 gun soon gave way to a 3in gun of higher velocity adapted for tank use, but even that would need to be replaced by a more powerful 90mm gun, at the expense of pace and protection, and in fact it was the action in the Ardennes that persuaded the military chiefs that this latter amendment was necessary.

Below: A 57mm anti-tank gun positioned on one of the many narrow tree-lined roads that gave the advantage to the defenders.

The M10, M18 and M36 tank destroyers all featured in the battle and here the Allies did have an advantage over their opponents; their German counterparts were less adaptable and unsuitable for much of the terrain over which the battle would be fought. The M10, with a 3in M7 gun mounted, offered manoeuvrability rather than protection. Because of its thin armour the sides and turret were sloped and angled in an endeavour to deflect shellfire.

The all-new M18 Hellcat had a similar profile to the German Panther, with the result that mis-identification was often a problem in murky conditions or by night. However it was lighter and faster than the M10 and its speed and manoeuvability often got the better of the heavier German armour.

The M36 tank destroyer was of a much more streamlined design, but such was its increased firepower, by means of an adapted 90mm anti-aircraft gun, that it proved too tempting an asset among US generals who were inclined to use it as a tank, only to discover that firepower counted for little in a lightly armoured and therefore susceptible battlefield machine.

Tanks and tank destroyers apart, the US troops used M3 half-tracks, 155mm self-propelled guns and 105mm howitzers; 40mm and 90mm anti-aircraft guns; .50cal Browning machine-guns for short-range targets; M2 60mm mortars used both to pound enemy positions at a range of up to one mile and to fire star shells to illuminate the battle area; and the M1 2.36in anti-tank rocket-launcher with a range of a quarter of a mile.

In the air P-47 Thunderbolts were used as fighter-bombers and some ageing A-20 Havocs, together with P-61s, flew with the night squadrons.

The American infantry were equipped with the Garand M1 semi-automatic rifle, the shorter-range M1 carbine and the Thompson M1 and M3 submachine-guns; on jeeps they were able to mount the M2. For close range and anti-personnel work, the troops were given basic, ancient fragmentation grenades and M9 rifle grenade-launchers.

GERMAN WEAPONS AND EQUIPMENT

For his Ardennes offensive, Hitler pressured his armaments suppliers to find 274 PzKpfw IV tanks and, while these were considered obsolete having been overtaken by the V Panther and VI Tigers, they were masters in their chosen environment and boasted better features than the Sherman. The 75mm gun was effective and only the squared sides and turret of the vehicle could be considered weaknesses.

The Panther design featured a high-velocity gun and the sloping design by now in vogue; it was faster but heavier, so the advantage of pace was not always seen on muddy or loose surfaces, but such was its design that it could often dominate from a static position.

The Tiger I brought with it a bigger gun (88mm) and enhanced armoured protection; just a handful were deployed in the Ardennes. The Tiger II was bigger and heavier still, a giant at 68 tons, but ponderous, with a top speed of just

21mph. It often had to avoid unmade roads and lightweight bridges and no more that forty-five saw action in this battle.

The German designers regularly sacrificed everything for increased power and protection, caring little for the effects on fuel consumption. The ramifications of this on any major advance are clear to see and the fuel shortage throughout Germany did not help.

The tank destroyers were inferior their American equivalents. Turretless, and forward-firing only, they were in truth no more than a 'big brother' to the assault guns which were more effective in the confines of Ardennes woods and valleys. For this reason, the Germans utilised various assault guns in this theatre; almost 300 were brought to the front. The machines had high-calibre front-facing guns that were capable of only minimal sideways movement. The need to face in the direction of fire was an obvious limitation.

Among lighter German vehicles in the Ardennes were half-tracked motorcycles, semi-tracked and half-tracked personnel carriers and artillery tow trucks, and a jeep-like vehicle, the Kübelwagen.

It was fortunate for the Allies, in the Ardennes and elsewhere, that the Germans failed to bring more of the mighty 88mm Pak 43/41 anti-tank guns to the battlefield. No Allied armour could withstand it, and its smaller partner, the 75mm Pak 40 was only marginally less impressive. For their medium guns they deployed the K18, but in the main had to use the First World War veteran, the 105mm M18 howitzer.

For protection against Allied aircraft, Hitler had allocated a meagre number of 88mm Flak 36 mobile guns, preferring to provide more field artillery in the shape of 150mm rocket-launchers and 80mm Granatwerfer 34 mortars. The disposable Panzerfaust 44 recoilless grenade-launcher was a truly valuable weapon at short range and the Germans also used rocket-launchers developed from captured American designs.

Personal weapons for the German infantryman in the Ardennes included the Mauser Kar 98k bolt-action rifle; the Schmeisser MP40 machine-pistol – a very much more advanced item, albeit with only a thirty-round capacity; the popular Sturmgewehr StG 44 assault rifle; the FG42 paratroop rifle and the rapid-firing MG42 machine-gun.

For grenades, the 'potato-masher' Stielhandgranate stick grenade was favoured. This intricately designed device was 'despatched' after the friction primer had set in train the explosion to take place four and a half seconds later.

5

THE BATTLE
THE PLANNING STAGE

Although the terrain of the Ardennes could scarcely be less suited to the tank warfare of 1944, Hitler was obsessed by the memory of his success in 1940, forgetting or ignoring the fact that then he had had fine summer weather, overwhelming air support and derisory opposition.

The question now was, would the ploy work again? Hitler was convinced that the Allies were at odds with one another and that if came to the crunch the Americans would break. On the other hand, gone were his legions of truly superb troops, with seemingly unlimited supplies of *matériel*, that had done his bidding in the days of his glory. Now there remained older men and boys bolstered by a few capable soldiers currently dispirited by defeat and retreat, but perhaps likely to be energised by the invitation to fight 'on the front foot' for a change. They would be opposed by tired but battle-hardened troops backed by a colossally powerful infrastructure.

Like most of his generals, the Führer was not by nature a defensive fighter. He had seldom called for anything other than swift and overwhelming attack. The wide range of military tactics that his senior soldiers might have learned at the *Kriegsakademie*, and the more cautious moves common to the battlefields of 1914–18, had been pushed firmly to the back of their minds, as their leader had urged them on during the years of undiluted success. It had been easy to please him in those days when they had everything they required and could set the agenda. In retreat, where astute defence, prudent withdrawal, and regrouping was necessary and delaying their opponents' progress was worthwhile, these commanders had, for the most part, been found wanting.

As it would turn out the planned offensive would see both sides implement almost every major land warfare strategy – certainly both armies would be required to exercise practical defence and withdrawal as well as advance and attack.

Hitler's bad health must surely be taken into account when examining the planning and directives of this beaten but defiant man who, clinging to unfounded beliefs, was convinced that he could still achieve military victory. It may be that at this juncture he was incapable of balancing the value of opening political negotiations against further battlefield losses.

The build-up to the Ardennes Offensive gave him a fresh focus, a positive to concentrate on rather than the negatives that had beset his campaign in the west since before D-Day. For the first time in weeks his inner group saw their leader energised rather than despondent, alert rather than dulled, studious in planning rather than ranting at setbacks, yet they cannot have been duped into believing that 'Wacht am Rhein' would prove the saving of the Third Reich.

From the day that the preparations had begun there was little or no chance of altering the Führer's mind. Orders were given for preparing the road and rail network to take mighty traffic; bridges had to be strengthened, track repaired and newly placed along highways, the locomotives themselves required armour-plating, river crossings and vessels needed modification. Massive additional quantities of ammunition and armoured and support vehicles had to be produced, and troops had to be brought in and trained for the task ahead.

The code-name 'Wacht am Rhein' was a rare piece of tactical astuteness on the part of Hitler – if it *was* his idea – since any intercepts of signals would suggest that the action was simply part of a defensive move to protect the German borders.

Now the German leader began to institute his own thinking within the overall plan. First came a discussion with the famed Otto Skorzeny, the SS major who had been tagged by the Allies as 'the most dangerous man in Europe' for his headline-grabbing exploits in, among other things, rescuing Mussolini and kidnapping the son of Admiral Horthy, the Hungarian leader. Without any consultation with his close advisers, Hitler instructed the special forces man to create his own brigade of specialists – they were to be SS commandos and paratroops – who could take part in a forthcoming great offensive in which they would be required to pose as Americans and, driving US vehicles, seizing bridges and spreading panic behind enemy lines. He gave the operation its own name – Operation 'Greif' – and made the blond adventurer a colonel!

As we have seen, Hitler had, remarkably, delayed sharing the details of the plan with his C-in-C West, von Rundstedt, or even with Walther Model who would command the entire Operation. Only late in the day were they allowed to receive copies of the Jodl-created scheme and their reaction was, as one might expect from two different but experienced military men, very similar: 'It cannot be done'.

Their endeavour to change Hitler's mind by presenting alternatives never had a hope of success, but both men felt they had to try, if only to defend their own reputation with their men and to give them a better chance of survival. The revision von Rundstedt came up with, code-named 'Martin', was less ambitious but remained founded on genuine Blitzkrieg techniques rather than Hitler's free interpretation of how they could be moulded to fit his dream. He suggested that Seventh Army in the south and Fifteenth Army in the north should work to protect thrusts by Fifth and Sixth Panzer Armies aimed at achieving the crossing of the Meuse and clearing trapped Allied forces. After this first stage he would review progress before taking the next step.

Model was equally cautious in seeking to strike a balance between the Führer's proclaimed preference and a more reasoned approach. He too proposed a sharp, narrow drive followed by a pause for evaluation, but he pressed for one movement to entrap the opposition in the Aachen salient, east of the Meuse, with sufficient reserves held back to allow for diverse options should the first stage bear fruit.

These two plans were discussed by their initiators with Dietrich, von Manteuffel and Brandenberger, commanders of the three armies concerned: Sixth Panzer, Fifth Panzer and Seventh Army. The agreed compromise took on board much of von Rundstedt's thinking but retained the more modest ambitions of Model's.

Those Allied forces that had penetrated the West Wall would be attacked and destroyed, the Germans would re-set their defences at the Meuse, and seek to capture Liège. It was certainly less ambitious than Hitler desired, but in the view of its presenters it offered a better chance of success and would see German forces on the offensive and regaining ground; they hoped this would satisfy their leader … but it was not to be.

On 1 November, just over three weeks before the Offensive was due to be mounted, Jodl sent the order to Westphal, von Rundstedt's Chief of Staff, and it contained scarcely any changes from Hitler's first idea. The start date was still 25 November, the three armies were still to attack the Allied line between Echternach and Monschau, with Dietrich's Sixth Panzer Army operating on the inside of the right-hand curve of the thrust and required to make most of the offensive strikes. The papers were marked in Hitler's own hand, *'Nicht abändern'* (No alterations).

Jodl's personal appearance at Army Group B HQ on 3 November gave the dissidents a further chance to voice their misgivings, but they had nothing new to say. They protested that the plan, even if successful in its earlier phases, would create a wide front which, in the expected weather and ground conditions and with the sparse men and equipment being promised, would be impossible to maintain for a sufficient period to neutralise the enemy divisions it was intended to trap. For his part, Jodl patiently explained that the Führer was determined to mount an offensive that would have impact, politically as well as militarily, and he held out no hope of compromise. This was endorsed once he had returned to see Hitler; his written reply was unequivocal: 'The operation is unalterable'.

As late as 23 November even the trusted Dietrich was daring to voice his doubts. At a meeting with Hitler and the other commanders he said that he was not sure that Sixth Panzer could do the job planned for them. This was before he realised that the roads designated for his men were often little better than dirt tracks and quite unsuitable for heavy vehicles. With the operation now becoming delayed until December when there was restricted daylight, a certainty of heavy fog and probably deep snow, he was convinced that the intended advances couldn't take place. Furthermore, the arrangements for fuel supply were haphazard; stocks, such as they were, remaining far behind the battle line and only able to be brought forward on congested, inadequate roads. For Hitler's most loyal servant among the leading commanders to be entering the fray with such misgivings was not a good sign even though, once he realised that there would be no changes, he sought to obey the instructions without dispute.

Thereafter only very small changes were made to the operational plan though, according to von Manteuffel in post-war discussions with Basil Liddell Hart, it was he who persuaded his leader to move the first attacks to dawn and stressed how vital it was to secure and hold the important road junction town of Bastogne.

THE SITUATION AT 16 DECEMBER

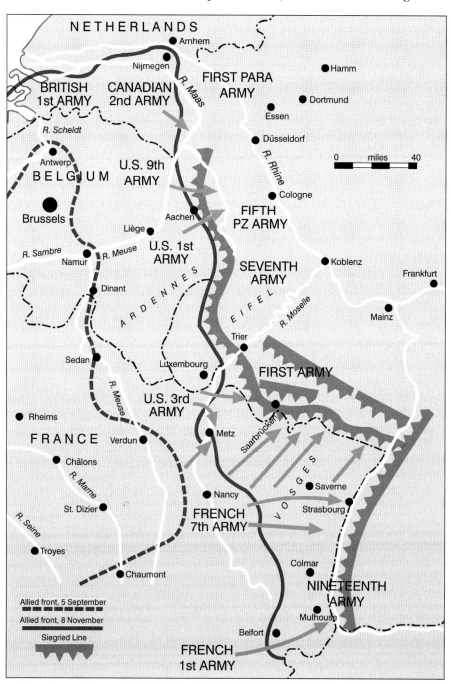

NETHERLANDS

Arnhem

Nijmegen

R. Maas

Hamm

FIRST PARA ARMY

Dortmund

Essen

Düsseldorf

R. Rhine

BRITISH 1st ARMY

CANADIAN 2nd ARMY

R. Scheldt

Antwerp

U.S. 9th ARMY

BELGIUM

Brussels

Cologne

Aachen

FIFTH PZ ARMY

Liège

U.S. 1st ARMY

R. Sambre

Namur

R. Meuse

Koblenz

Frankfurt

SEVENTH ARMY

Dinant

ARDENNES

EIFEL

R. Moselle

Mainz

Trier

Sedan

Luxembourg

FIRST ARMY

R. Meuse

U.S. 3rd ARMY

Rheims

Metz

Saarbrücken

FRANCE

Verdun

Châlons

R. Marne

V O S G E S

Saverne

Nancy

Strasbourg

St. Dizier

FRENCH 7th ARMY

R. Seine

Troyes

Colmar

Chaumont

NINETEENTH ARMY

Mulhouse

Allied front, 5 September

Belfort

Allied front, 8 November

Siegried Line

FRENCH 1st ARMY

0   miles   40

Hitler allocated von Rundstedt sixty-four divisions, but, as we have established, they did not comprise troops of the same calibre as those available to Eisenhower, who had sixty-five divisions; given personnel of equal quality it could be argued that a closer contest might have been possible. The equation can be described as follows: the Germans had better tanks but fewer of them, with fewer reserve personnel and weaker logistics, and had not fought offensively for some time; the Allies boasted more battlefield equipment, the enthusiasm generated by their successes since the Normandy beaches and reasonable reserves and logistical support, but were somewhat weary from their long advance through France. Both sides would have expected air support, but Hitler had reckoned that the weather would prohibit extensive advantage being gained from that quarter. The theory of this balance sheet would suggest that the advantage of surprise was crucial; if it could be employed correctly and ruthlessly, how well would the Allies respond?

The practical truth was less simple than this analysis for it is clear that too much of the German plan was based on unfounded enthusiasm and unjustified promises. The Germans would come to the first day of the offensive with uncertain, sceptical battlefield leadership while the Allies boasted confident generals who, despite differences of opinion, were committed to getting the job done and had an expectation of victory based on their recent triumphs. At troop level this would be a battle between well-organised battle-hardened, well-equipped victors and a hotchpotch of a few skilled soldiers and reservists, of whom the latter were mostly too young or too old and whose performance in the face of battle could fall short of what was needed.

The Allied front in the Ardennes sector was justifiably lightly manned compared to elsewhere, with just a handful of divisions and some reconnaissance units along this 80-mile sector. Despite their being aware of the 1940 precedent – perhaps they should have taken this more into account – the Allied commanders had every reason to suppose that, in the unlikely event of the enemy choosing to mount any counter at this time – in midwinter and with suspect logistics – they would surely pick suitable, especially more open, ground where their potent tanks could support swift straight attack. Bradley admitted to knowing the details of the 1940 blitz through the region. but considered it an acceptable risk to leave this sector of the front lightly defended.

Not all his officers were in accord with this. General Alan Jones, commanding 106th Division, was one who expressed concern about the increased armoured movements among the Germans manning their defences just beyond his most forward troops. The staff supporting his superior, General Troy Middleton of VIII Corps, were dismissive of Jones' reports and even joked that the Germans were probably playing records of moving armour so as to scare his men.[4] General Courtney Hodges, commander of First Army, was another to receive adverse reports, his Intelligence officer, Colonel Dickson, avidly predicting that there could be a German attack through the Ardennes at any time. But apart from these examples of nervousness and a few comments from German residents in the area of the front, no one on the Allied side of the divide was expecting any widespread action for the time being. All were convinced it was they, not their opponents, who would make the next move and that this would be when General Eisenhower gave the word. He, incidentally, was in faraway Versailles and would be spending the evening of 15 December celebrating his elevation to five star general before having talks with Bradley the following day as well as attending the wedding of his orderly.

Hitler was certainly aware, by means of intelligence and communication intercepts, of how thin the Allied line was, but for him this was just one reason to pick the Ardennes; he truly relished the idea of tempting providence by repeating 1940 and the selection of an unlikely point of attack was all part of his core strategy … surprise.

To reach the Meuse from their start point, the German units would need to travel some forty plus miles and then a further sixty or more to reach Antwerp. This was a tough demand in any circumstances, particularly those afflicting the German commanders, but it was especially so when fog, frost, snow and cling-ing mud could be expected. Furthermore, though much of the Ardennes pro-vided good cover from air attack and would certainly assist in maintaining the surprise element, it was susceptible to blocked roads and tracks – by accidental and deliberate means – and the hills above the roads through the area were ideal positions for an enemy employing defensive tactics.

The triangle formed by the River Rhine and the West Wall was deeper close to the Ardennes and the Luxembourg border than in most other sectors. This would enable the German build-up to take place across territory they controlled and which was not currently threatened. The Allies had pushed furthest forward to the south of the Ardennes and Eifel hills around Metz, and to the north past Liège and Aachen.

If we have already established that the Germans were as well prepared for the offensive as they could be and that the Allies were, at the very least, less ready than they should have been, we must acknowledge here that there were other factors that contributed to this being a prime time for Hitler to make his move. The Allied military leaders had become frustrated by delays and reversals not just at Antwerp and Arnhem, but also in their Italian Campaign, the Far East and China. Furthermore, while the attitude in Washington was still one of a certain contentment, the politicians in Great Britain, led by a fretful Churchill, saw only setbacks to add to their gloom about the nation's parlous financial state and the impending election. In the event it was the American commander, Omar Bradley, who would bear the brunt of the criticism of lack of preparedness on the part of the Allied forces facing the German advance.

It was Bradley who had been adamant in his dismissal of any likelihood of German attacks, though Montgomery, even on the day they began, was also reporting the enemy as being unable to mount any offensive moves. Typically of tactically astute military men, they put themselves in the position of the enemy and assessed the position. The Germans, they were sure, had irreparable shortages of men, guns and tanks, air support, ammunition and fuel. In that position, they would not wage war so neither, they assumed, would their opponent. That Great Britain and her allies had been making too many assumptions about the behaviour and plans of the Führer for six years of war, let alone the years prior to 1939, counted for little now as the combined Allied forces patrolled a huge front between them and a demoralised nation and its spent military forces.

Furthermore, General Bradley could not see what Hitler would gain by pushing the Allies back towards, or to, the Meuse. Both he and other commanders expressed the view that such an attack would not only be foolish on the part of the Germans but an advantage to the Allied commanders and their men. A weak, futile offensive by the Germans would simply play into Bradley's hands; he could surely annihilate any forces breaking through at any point of the front and do so at a time of his own choosing when they had over-stretched their supply lines, run out of ammunition or equipment or both, or simply realised their folly. If there was any nervousness in the American camp at all it was that the weather could damage the superiority of Allied air power and make the ground conditions exceedingly unpleasant and thus affect their own plans for advance; George Patton actually asked his chaplain to pray for better weather!

But, such conjecture was not part of daily Allied strategy meetings ... it just was not going to happen.

THE BUILD-UP

The crucial element of the Ardennes Offensive was surprise; it had no chance of success if the Allies were alerted to the German plan. Hitler's ruse in giving the operation a name that suggested defence rather than attack was one of his wiser acts and the fact that men and equipment could be moved to the front across country that neither Allied ground forces nor aircraft presently covered was to his benefit. But getting the attackers to their forward positions was a monumental task.

If the first day of the attack was to achieve its objective, in surroundings that were not conducive to swift, clinical forward movement, everyone and everything had to be at the 'departure gate' on time.

The date of 25 November had been discarded and Hitler was now privately committed to 16 December, though only his closest staff members knew of this date and he had yet to brief his generals. He was receiving daily forecasts from his meteorologists to assess when the weather might be at its worst and thus deprive the Allies of their air advantage. By 11 December, of the three participating armies, Seventh was chiefly in place, Fifth Panzer was short of only one panzer division – though, in the event, it remained so until after the commencement of action – and Sixth Panzer was complete. Between 12 and 15 December all units edged into their final battle positions to await Hitler's order to proceed. Much of the movement was undertaken at night with, towards the end of the exercise, the panzer armies' assault troops moving through the Army Group B lines together with the leading infantry sections and artillery and rocket batteries.

To arrange this collection of forces would have been a mighty task of organisation at any time but, at this point, it was a remarkable achievement. For Germany to have mustered sufficient logistical muscle even to begin the task, with relatively few errors and omissions, was a tribute to the skill of the German Army and the continuing readiness to implement orders promptly and effectively. Such effort required considerable confidence that instructions would be carried out and passed on through the ranks without demur and with the utmost clarity, but on this occasion it had the added requirement of extreme secrecy. For the plans to be kept from the enemy, these movements had to be conducted without fuss or drama and in a manner that suggested nothing more than a build-up of defensive lines. Road surfaces were strewn with straw to muffle the noise of tank tracks, bridging units likely to be needed in the advance were secluded in hedgerows and under trees, and many of the stores of ammunition were brought forward on foot to limit the need for motorised transport.

The strict employment of the agreed plan for the build-up certainly meant that the Germans prevented the Allies interpreting the moves as part of an offensive. Secrecy was retained in movements and broadcasts; the measured forward routing did not suggest rush or panic. If the Allied officers allowed themselves to preclude any chance of a German offensive and thus become relaxed as they paused ahead of their own attacks, the ability to get to the state of readiness at the front line without being noticed by the opposition air force or Intelligence teams was still an astonishing feat. It registers all the more when the statistics are shown: twenty divisions with 250,000 men, more than 15,000 tons of ammunition, 3.17 million gallons of fuel, and yet more of everything – though perhaps still not enough – held in reserve farther back. In addition, the troops had had to be brought from different fronts and locations, many by the Reichsbahn system that had been up to the task despite the best efforts of the Allied airmen. Some 140,000 tons of *matériel* were taken to the front by 500 supply trains, and more than 1,500 convoys brought up troops by road.

Remember, this was Hitler gathering everything he could, from wherever he could locate it, by whatever means it took, in order to launch his great counter-attack. Whether or not the actual military strategy was fatally flawed from the outset, the preparations were, if not perfect, not the reason for failure.

It begs the question: could Allied Intelligence have not performed better? Some have suggested that the Ardennes was akin to Pearl Harbor in terms of an Intelligence nightmare, but none has been able to identify one culprit, or even a few, for the basic problem appears to be the state of calm confidence that pervaded Allied, and particularly American, thinking at the time. From the end of the summer the view had been that Allied victory was assured and could be achieved as and when they chose; there was absolutely no expectation of a German counter-thrust. The recall of von Rundstedt and the strengthening of the West Wall defences intrigued and frustrated but did nothing to dent the optimism; if anything, it lulled the Allies into a greater sense of false security as they looked for von Rundstedt's hand in all German moves on the front and they knew him to be cautious and traditional in his military tactical thinking. One can be critical of those charged with studying Adolf Hitler as a ruler and army commander that they could not believe that he, rather than any of his experienced and talented military commanders, was setting the policy and issuing the orders. They could not see von Rundstedt doing anything more than securing his defences as best he could; had they imagined Hitler as the architect, and studied the early years of the war more readily, perhaps they might have been more ready to consider that German attack might be an option. As it was, the perceived conditions were not those that saw Intelligence staff on high alert; this was to be a prime example of Intelligence gathering being one thing, correct interpretation being a wholly different matter.

Such Intelligence reports as were issued spoke, correctly, of what the enemy could and could not do, and of his general capabilities. So the reports were of low German morale and forces incapable of anything other than robust defence, though the observation was made that Sixth Panzer Army did not appear to be operational at any point and predictions of its location were just that … guesses and surmise. They could only be sure that this armoured reserve force would come out of hiding when 'we [the Allies] attack', and it was not, of course, their job to decide when this would be. Major-General Sir Kenneth Strong, Eisenhower's head of Intelligence, had a good knowledge of the German Army, its structure and methods and he did indicate that there was a possibility of an attack through the Ardennes at any time that six days of continual bad weather could nullify Allied aircraft. So, in this aspect he did issue warnings, but why were they not heeded?

In the days immediately prior to the German moves, Strong and his staff knew that Fifth Army was assembling between Koblenz and Cologne and reported this, but they did so with insufficient strength and detail to persuade Bradley and Eisenhower to act against their own soldiering instincts. Fighting experience versus Intelligence theory was also in evidence more locally where front line units of the 28th and 106th Infantry Divisions advised of increased armour activity just across from them, and local residents offered various reports about seeing more German equipment that ever before. When these observations were considered serious enough to be sent back to regional headquarters, they were treated with a lack of concern as were the results of interrogation of new German prisoners who actually told of an attack and gave the date, 16 December. The latter was taken as being meant to mislead!

So, in part, the Intelligence failing was due to the reluctance of the generals to accept somewhat superficial evidence, blandly presented, over their own feelings, based on what they had inflicted on the enemy during the previous months, that the Germans were a weakened and demoralised force incapable of significant offensive action. When an Intelligence officer is asked to 'prove it' and he is only acting on reports that may be deliberately vague or themselves based on second-hand comments or be corrupt, this specialist can be too cautious for the overall good. Being responsible for setting in motion a decision to commit thousands of men to battle is a daunting prospect, but perhaps Strong and his team could have pressed their case harder.

It is only fair to mention that, as Hitler wanted, the days leading up to the offensive had seen persistent mists and low cloud prohibiting many reconnaissance flights that might have returned with hard evidence of troop and armour movements. Previously, however, such flights had told of increased rail activity and of long enemy convoys on roads heading west; these, perhaps because of Allied knowledge of an impending operation called 'Watch on the Rhine', were taken to be units being transported to shore up the West Wall.

On 15 December the Intelligence maps at 12 Army Group HQ showed no moves on the part of the opposition. For the sector of the front from Monschau to the Moselle they showed only five German divisions, with a sixth seemingly moving back away from the front near the Schnee Eifel.

Only now, a few hours before the attack, were the troops briefed on the details of the advance. The plan devised by Hitler and High Command, rather than von Rundstedt as the Allies believed, had only been explained to his generals three days before and now the front-line commanders were given their orders. In summary, the main effort would be made by Dietrich's Sixth Panzer Army on the northern, or inner, border of a large right-hand curve through the Ardennes to Antwerp. He was to cross the Meuse around Liège, head for the Albert Canal and continue broadening his front from Maastricht to Antwerp; provisional protection of his right flank would have to come from his own infantry divisions. Von Manteuffel's Fifth Panzers would shadow Dietrich's moves to his south, curving around below him and covering his left and rear lines by governing a line through Antwerp, Brussels, Namur and Dinant. Below von Manteuffel at the initial breakout would be Brandenberger's Seventh Army which would anchor the base of the giant curving drive by covering its border on an angle formed by the rivers Semois and Meuse.

Before we start to view the action, let us give a final consideration of the main German commanders for what was Hitler's great last gamble. Von Rundstedt was but a figurehead for the operation and a reluctant one at that. It was important that the massed ranks of experienced and novice German soldiers believed the veteran was involved and supportive, and no bad thing that the Allies believed this too. It must have irritated Hitler greatly that this was the case, that the Allies would give more respect to a plan they believed was hatched by a military master than an egotistical dictator. Had the old Prussian been given more freedom to conduct the campaign his way – and remember he thought the plan was brilliant in some aspects – the Ardennes offensive would have been limited to regaining some ground, giving the Allies a short, sharp shock and testing their resolve. Had von Rundstedt operated to his plan the Germans might have got to the Meuse, without ambition to go further, and might have given Eisenhower a new situation to grapple with, perhaps negotiate over.

Walther Model was a skilled commander and a committed Nazi. Though not a member of the Führer's inner circle, he was admired by that group for his ability to get results by dint of extracting full effort from every man. Where von Rundstedt was a planner and a marshal of policy, Model was a 'doer' and an avid battlefield visitor, where he was as likely to be seen directing troop movement and deployment when von Rundstedt would delegate and remain, as a rule, well behind the scenes. Both men viewed the 'Wacht am Rhein' scheme as undeliverable; Model, because of his political loyalty was prepared to manage it as best he could.

In theory, Sepp Dietrich had also had a fine military career and there was little doubt about his courage and commitment to the cause, but he was no master of the detail of war, of its logistics, or its craft … he commanded by gut reaction as might be expected of a former butcher. He could not explain his thinking and his reputation gained on the Eastern Front and in Normandy came from his rousing calls to arms rather than any considered disposition of forces. He was a fanatical supporter of Hitler's and owed his status to the leader. With so many of the candidates for leadership of Sixth Panzer under suspicion after the July bomb plot, Dietrich was a dependable choice, at least in the eyes of the man making the appointment!

Below: Amid the common clinging mud of an Ardennes field, American soldiers struggle to reposition an anti-tank gun.

In contract, Hasso von Manteuffel was of the von Rundstedt mould. From sound Prussian stock and steeped in solid military tradition, he won promotion through impressive leadership performances in North Africa and Russia and, though his appearance gave no hint of dynamism or physical strength, he was a soldier's soldier who engendered whole-hearted support from the ranks. Of independent mind and spirit, he was still admired by Hitler; even his ambivalence towards the Nazi cause did not hinder his rise to the top.

Of this quartet two were utterly committed to the cause for which they fought, three had every right through their qualifications to be involved, and one would quickly find himself 'out of his depth' in so complex a battle-zone. None had faith in the project they were implementing, though, again, probably two fervently wanted it to succeed.

THE ACTION BEGINS

We should remind ourselves that the German plan was to be at the Meuse in two days and Antwerp in six and that the two primary elements of the offensive were surprise and speed. Because of the limited resources available to Hitler and his reluctance to involve any of the senior battlefield commanders in the planning, the scheme lacked flexibility. It is the nature of warfare, perhaps especially in the circumstances we find here, that theoretical plans quickly founder on the needs of practical action; the finest battlefield commanders, as we see later in the contest, are those who can think on their feet, adapting their thinking as the situation requires, and have men and equipment at hand to implement their thinking. Hitler's plan of campaign was rigid; he felt it needed to be to stand any chance of success and to keep his commanders and troops focused. There was no fall-back scheme, no room for manoeuvre, and, in truth, no acceptance that there could be any reversal of fortune that would call for a change to the plan.

With only the obliging Jodl and Keitel at his side, and von Rundstedt out of the picture in respect of any contribution to setting the Ardennes strategy, the Führer had no 'sounding board' to raise doubts and devise secondary tactics if needed. Von Rundstedt's late intervention, and Hitler's brusque rejection of his alternative scheme, may have unnerved those present, and certainly Model and von der Heydte had the gravest misgivings, while von Manteuffel could never equate the intended pace of progress with the conditions that would obtain. Optimism, blind or otherwise, was in short supply and seen only in the likes of Dietrich, whose career-long support for his leader had been stretched to breaking point in the build-up before he was persuaded to back the initiative.

So, on that night of 15 December 1944, the American and British forces forming the Allied front were considering battle but not expecting one. They knew it was only a matter of time before Eisenhower gave the signal for the push into Germany and on to Berlin. At command levels the officers were conscious of the alternative plans being considered, a few were aware of the debates taking place in London and Washington, but the simple artilleryman and his infantry counterpart were resting, waiting and preparing for the next part of their great advance, taking the war back to the Third Reich.

Among the ranks of the Allied troops manning the Ardennes sector the atmosphere was even more relaxed; these were men who had been given a quiet part of the front in which to get their bearings and become acquainted with the now severe weather, or units that had been given time and space to recuperate after a particularly strenuous time of intense action. The Ardennes in winter does not equate to relaxing holiday conditions, but by comparison, this was the comfortable and calm sector of the wide Allied front line. Between Monschau, south of Aachen, and the Moselle north-east of Luxembourg, III Corps in the south, V Corps in the north and VIII Corps in the centre beneath and around Schnee Eifel, were attending to their own well-being and making ready for when the call came. Their patrols were modest and unspectacular, the most forward units in foxholes, sheds and farm outhouses, cast only an occasional eye towards the German troops across the gap between the combatants; until the last few days there had been little to observe or hear.

Troy Middleton, commanding VIII Corps, was aware that he had next to no reserves, but he had been given no reason to suppose that he needed any; the men and equipment he had were enough. It was, in the words of a participant, Robert Merriam, [5] 'a ghost front, a phoney sector'. He also spoke of taking casual drives in a jeep close to the front line which indicates just how quiet it was at this point.

By comparison with the Americans, the pent-up energy at the sharp end of the assembled German ranks was dramatically apparent for here were the best of the soldiers the German nation could muster for this action, and they were buoyed up by the prospect of taking the offensive again, and stirred by messages from Hitler, von Rundstedt and Jodl. The older men and youths drawn in to swell the numbers were, in the main, among the second echelon of forces waiting for the 'off'. None of the rank and file in the German front line would have known that the strategy in which they were about to be deployed came not from von Rundstedt, their solid veteran war leader, but from the manic mind of a physically weak and mentally ailing Führer.

16 DECEMBER

Thus it was that as the first rays of dawn considered making an appearance in the skies above the Schnee Eifel on 16 December, the silence was about to be broken. Initially the skies echoed only to the roar of V1s overhead. Noisy, yes, disruptive, yes, but not worthy of more than a momentary acknowledgement by the American units beneath as the destinations of the missiles were beyond their positions. But the purpose of these flights was principally to drown the sounds of early movement on the part of the ground troops who, at 0500, had already been weaving through the wooded valleys unnoticed and unheard. It was now that the 2,000 German guns opened up to give the slumbering opposition the fiercest wake-up call imaginable. Targeting American positions as they did, the arrival of the barrage was a genuinely rude awakening!

With minimal barrages into the villages of Roth and Kobscheid, because advance troops were already there and the American defenders were few and far between, the targets of the fusillade were a little farther back. The sky around them suddenly echoed to the sundry shrieks, thumps and hisses of diverse launches of artillery. Seconds later the trees shook and cracked, tents were plastered with shrapnel and worse, and the ground vibrated like a malfunctioning mattress. It was now that the Intelligence reports had all the accuracy of a clock without its mechanism.

On the German front line the infantry waited impatiently for the artillery barrage to lift, and the officers were poised for the moment to give their next dramatic orders. Many had never witnessed German armour in the ascendancy, on the offensive; their hearts must have skipped several beats.

On the American side, many thought that this was the sound of their own guns firing in accordance with some directive of which they had not been informed, but this interpretation was short lived. Faint amusement at the sound of enemy artillery action quickly gave way to concern that it was so concentrated and mixed. Then there was worry, next there was alarm and, within seconds, some panic. But the first reaction of many of the American troops in their foxholes and makeshift shelters was one of puzzlement as much as alarm. This dank morning, with mist clinging determinedly to the hills and weaving eerily though the valleys, seemed unlikely to witness a major initiative. Perhaps this was just a sharp reminder that the war was not yet won; perhaps the German artillery hereabouts had just received new ammunition supplies and wanted to let the enemy know that they, the Americans, might be resting but the opposition was not.

If these were the first thoughts it is entirely understandable, if they brought momentary paralysis it would be expected, but they were soon changed because the barrage was to be quickly followed by panzer troops and grenadiers employing their prized element of surprise with great élan.

Some distance behind the lines, junior officers were awoken by the barrage but were initially calm. Farther back, their seniors were oblivious, and remained dozing in their HQ while contemplating another easy day of forward planning and assessment.

The Losheim Gap, the Wehrmacht's route into France in 1940, was again the focal point, and above it, atop the Schnee Eifel, the forward units of the Allied defenders were already without telephone lines and finding their wireless wavelengths jammed by German music. Already the villages just behind the Allied line and in front of the River Our were being hit, but despite the frustration of being unable to communicate with the rear and perhaps the suddenness of the onslaught and the inexperience of some of the troops, there was still no panic; all their briefings on the current situation led them to believe that this was no more than the opposition flexing their muscles … a local initiative.

The expected brevity of the attack proved a false hope. It went on, and on, for thirty minutes, then forty-five, and soon towns well beyond the Our were being reached, including Clervaux, some four miles from the German lines. The troops in each of the small forward units felt that they alone were being singled out; those in Monschau and Höfen to the very north of the threatened sector were oblivious to what was happening in Losheim and Roth, either side of Krewinkel in the Losheim Gap, and they in turn were ignorant of the action farther south around Ouren, Roder and Weiler. Each sector of the Front thought it was facing its own little fight.

For more than an hour this was war at a distance but then, in the north of the sector, it was the turn of Sepp Dietrich's Sixth Panzer Army to make it personal as the artillery onslaught ceased and these experienced units attacked the 99th Division's positions to the accompaniment of an overflight by the new jet aircraft. Despite his pre-battle boasts, the untried nature of the opposition, and other advantages that he had started with, Dietrich was unable to ride roughshod over the sparse opposition. Sixth Panzer had been allocated 90 Mark VI Tiger Tanks among its firepower, but the infantry lacked assault guns and went onto the attack with insufficient trained engineer companies; this deficit would soon make itself felt. Remarkably resourceful action by his ragbag opponents slowed down Dietrich's advance. In fact it can be argued that the resolute and sponta-neous defence by sundry small groups of the Americans' patrolling units won the Battle of the Ardennes in the first four days. They had not been prepared to withstand an onslaught, and there were incidences of dreadful confusion and, perhaps, cowardice, but given the suddenness of the attack, most of Bradley's men showed great fortitude in delaying the German advance, and this played havoc with Hitler's time scale.

Ironically, given that the American forces were spread so thinly on the ground, their greatest concentration was precisely where the Germans needed their speediest advance, on the inside of the giant curve of attack that would take them towards Antwerp. This area, around the Elsenborn Ridge, was occupied by fair numbers of General Gerow's 2nd and 99th Infantry Divisions in V Corps because some of them had been involved in offensive action against the Roer dams prior to the German initiative. And however adept their opponents were at operating through the terrain of thick woodland, rocky gorges with streams and inadequate roads, the Americans had at least become well acquainted with it in the previous weeks.

But if the crack units of Dietrich's panzers were being held south of Monschau, the drive into the Losheim Gap itself was altogether more purpose-ful and effective. Tanks and support vehicles quickly negotiated static obstacles and thrust through the infantry lines of the opposition like a knife through butter. The tenuous link between 99th Division and 14th Cavalry Group was broken, only the barest of alarm calls reaching their respective HQs. The forward Allied positions, in places only reached by cart paths and forest firebreaks, were so intermittent and sparsely manned, that the defenders would have been lucky to prevent a stray deer passing through their lines let alone a panzer formation.

Various groups managed to consolidate and bring to a halt some of the panzer groups, and it was about now, some time after 0700, that a few messages were reaching HQ some miles back. The news was imprecise and contradictory: '… heavy fire barrage' … five tanks – no, more'… 'and now panzer troops' …. 'tanks and armoured cars' … 'contact with the enemy, returning fire'.

Forces under the command of von Manteuffel were sweeping past the minimal defences in the Gap and pushing on past Roth, towards Manderfeld and Weckerath, and on down the valley towards the larger village of Schönberg in the south of the Gap, and some ten miles beyond the point where they had left the West Wall defences; the Allied salient at this point was already under severe threat. Here 28th Division, one of the groups posted to this area for rest and recuperation, was now holding a crucial sector of the Front. Although German infantry had crossed the River Our in some places before the main attack in order to prepare the route for the larger force, this advance team had been severely dealt with, suffering many losses before having to withdraw, but elsewhere the news was bad for the Americans with the road to Bastogne and the Meuse now opened up by early infantry teams. Dozens of American positions became cut off, at Kobschied for example, and minimal garrisons were appalled to see enemy forces approaching that outnumbered them ten- or twenty-fold.

At Krewinkel, the easternmost point of the American line, the excellent defensive position enabled the first wave of confident German attacks to be seen off by heavy and accurate fire, but later attacks enabled some German troops to get into the town before being forced to withdraw in the face of further resolute defence and innovative sniping initiatives.

As we shall establish, there were many failures in the German plans, examples of lost opportunities and missed timings. Already the all-powerful tanks that were to follow these infantry pushes from the Our crossing at Dasburg had failed to appear because sections of the bridge for the heavy armour had arrived here in the wrong order. The resulting traffic jam on the narrow roads down into the valley from the German side was holding up a fundamental element of the forward drive in this sector, though the delay would soon be resolved. Elsewhere, previous demolition work undertaken by the Germans in their retreat behind the West Wall defences, was now hindering their progression because not enough temporary construction material had been brought to the sector.

At Buchholtz station, just a mile through the most forward American defensive lines, shortly after the artillery barrage had ended, an early party of German infantry was almost past the defending Americans before they were recognised and repulsed. About 75 of the enemy were killed during a morning of close-quarter fire fights. This caused some German units planning to use the route to seek another road to the north-east and such stubborn resistance brought about similar ill-discipline all along the front, leading to primary attack locations becoming cluttered and established priorities ignored. Despite this, the 'Wacht am Rhein' operation was certainly belying its defensive connotations; at least the Americans in the front line were sure by now that this was an *offensive* in every possible way. Most forward positions were being by-passed or knocked aside, and by midday the entire Allied front knew it was under severe attack, even if the full story had still not been relayed back to regional headquarters let alone the senior commanders, and the troops in some sectors still believed that they were the only ones suffering. What was also certain was that the local population was alive to the threat of a new invasion by the German forces that had been driven from their land and villages just a few weeks before.

Soon the story of the morning was finally reaching Allied Command Posts. Villages in the Losheim Gap were being evacuated by residents and American forces alike with Manderfeld, Holzheim and Wischeid among those villages passed without a fight. If action was not taken quickly, Schönberg, a target for von Manteuffel's infantrymen, would come under threat, and the important road junction of St-Vith lay just six miles on from there. The Americans were soon to find that von Manteuffel had other units heading in that direction from south of the Schnee Eifel via the unprotected hamlet of Bleialf so the forward teams of 106th Division on the Eifel hills were likely to be cut off.

Once the débâcle of the Dasburg crossing had been resolved the 200 tanks and tens of thousands of men due to cross at this point were unlikely to meet much resistance before they reached the town of Clervaux some five miles on from the river. The attractive town and its environs were in the hands of 110th Regiment, but the dawn bombardment had accounted for much of their communications system and foot messengers were now racing back to Colonel Hurley Fuller's HQ to tell of tanks and men and even horse-drawn vehicles having been seen in the valleys around Marnach. And this was only one sector of the front; the picture was repeated at many points and the attacking German forces could now be seen by American observer aircraft.

The response of the American front line soldiers was varied. Some stood and fought, and repulsed the enemy, others were so unexpectedly caught by superior numbers that they were forced to withdraw rapidly; many lost their lives. The chaos of retreating men and armour amidst panic-stricken locals fearful of a new German occupation prevented some officers getting forward to assess the position of their units. By midday in the Losheim Gap, for example, large numbers of infantry had followed the assault troops across the Our and widespread instructions to withdraw were reaching some by-passed units. As soon as the forces behind the front were alerted to create new defences and roadblocks, such as at Holzheim, they found these places already overrun and unreachable.

The most senior commanders of the Allied forces had spent the first six hours of Hitler's offensive almost oblivious of the serious events taking place miles to the east. Bradley was with Eisenhower in Versailles, having driven there from Luxembourg during the morning to attend a conference on infantry planning. It was early evening when the meeting was interrupted by a message telling of a German attack at five points in First Army's section. Omar Bradley's first reaction was that this was a spoiling attack in response to Patton's activity in the south, but Eisenhower was having none of it. For him it was illogical for a local attack to be set against the part of the Allied Front that was least well manned.

He immediately decided to send General Troy Middleton two divisions to help stem the advance: 7th Armored under Robert Hasbrouck from a rest area near Aachen and 10th Armored from Patton's Army. He gave Bradley the unenviable task of telling George Patton that he was to lose these men and the latter was typically robust in his argument against such a move for he, like Bradley, accepted the Intelligence view that the Germans were incapable of mounting a major attack and therefore this had to be a simple and futile flexing of muscles. Bradley forced the decision on Patton and arranged for Ninth Army's 7th Armored to be brought down. Those required to move had no better idea of what was truly taking place on the German border than anyone else, though Eisenhower's prompt reaction certainly gave those in attendance good reason to get fresh defences in

Below: Knocked-out US Sherman tanks during the battle.

place; at this point there was no desire to follow Patton's edict that a German attack should be allowed to take place so that the superior Allied forces could cut off and annihilate those participating.

St-Vith was to feature prominently in the Ardennes Offensive. A cosmopolitan settlement housing both Belgians and Germans, it formed the hub of a network of roads that splayed out towards Malmédy and then Liège in the north, Lutzkampen and then Luxembourg in the south and, crucially, Bastogne – another centre of the road network – to the south-west and Dinant and Brussels to the west; it was central to the early German breakthrough, both geographically and strategically. At this time it housed the command post of Major General Alan Jones, commander of 106th Infantry Division. By mid-afternoon on 16 December Jones had problems; he knew his men nearer the border had suffered some attacks, but he did not know the severity of the offensive nor that St-Vith was a focal point of it. Although he made connection with Middleton and was told that 7th Armored was being sent to his aid, the line was bad and he thought that his orders were to leave his front-line units in place whereas Middleton believed that he had clearly got the message across that Jones should withdraw the troops he felt were most vulnerable.

The lull in the fighting that came as darkness approached did not see a reduction of planning and discussion on the part of the Americans, all of whom were new to taking defensive measures and had not expected to be tested in this respect. Each was trying to get more news, more men, more time.

A battlefield general needs knowledge of the action zone in order to effect the right decision-making. An opponent removes the chance of this awareness by means of surprise. The combination of tight security and well-planned secretive build-up and the poor quality of Allied, especially American, Intelligence, now contrived to leave the Allied command bereft of knowledge from top to bottom. One day into the battle they still had very little idea of the scope of the attack or its ultimate goal.

The right-curving German drive saw Dietrich's Sixth Panzer Army alongside von Manteuffel's Fifth Panzers at the Losheim Gap where the commands met. While Dietrich's teams to the north of his sector had not enjoyed complete success, his units in the Gap were almost to the point where they could arc west and north along planned routes; von Manteuffel was due to make for St-Vith and beyond and had every confidence he could do so. Because of the delays the Germans were facing north of Losheim, Major General Gerow felt that he had made good moves to reinforce his V Corps defensive teams, but he was still to get clear reports from the Gap so had actually been sending more men into a position where they could become cut off. It was only when retreating forces arrived, flooding out to the north of the Gap, through Holzheim to Honsfeld, that the situation became clearer.

But not all German moves had gone to plan. Continuing logistic errors caused delays and certain elements of first-day action had not been implemented. Because bridge parts had not arrived, tanks had broken down or American resistance had not been dealt with, some planned action was now seven hours overdue. Jochen Peiper and his 1st SS Panzer Division had, for example, been delayed by German military traffic jams and chose to divert along a route not scheduled to be used; this injudicious gamble, made in anger, saw him lose six tanks to German mines that had not been cleared. The cavalier SS lieutenant-colonel reached Lanzerath by midnight but was still separated from his intended route through Honsfeld by heavily mined woodland lanes.

Another highly motivated leader who had a specific task to complete was Otto Skorzeny and he was also delayed by various German-induced delays. His brigade of American impressionists had not reached their goal and he had no option but to wait with his three battle groups for the route to clear. Perhaps he should have spent the time teaching these men, kitted out with accurate American uniforms and equipment, more about American history and culture for it was their failings in tests on these subjects that ruined their disguise and ultimate effectiveness once Allied forces became alerted to the presence within American lines of the very few finally deployed on this mission. Hitler's personal plan for Skorzeny and his men would prove no more than a minor irritant in the early days of the battle and, in truth, it was a waste of the talents of this pioneer special forces exponent.

At the end of the first day, the balance of achievement was held by the Germans, and by some considerable margin. The vital element of surprise had been achieved to a dramatic degree and good advances made. Some border towns remained in American hands, though some of these had been by-passed, and the response of the attackers turned defender had been sporadic with heroic defence at some locations and abject panic at others. Eisenhower's early response to move troops to the threatened areas was correct, but could not bring immediate relief. Close to the front the middle ranking American officers had been too confused and ill-informed to react as the textbooks said they should. By midnight on this first day one thing was certain, most Americans, including Eisenhower at Versailles, knew that this was no side-show; Hitler was carrying the fight back across his borders and into Allied territory.

Gerd von Rundstedt was at the 'Adlerhorst' and was doing his best to ensure that Hitler did not simply focus on the better news from the front. He showed his pessimism for the whole venture by rejecting any idea of switching the weight of the attack farther south to compensate Dietrich's sluggish start – though this was a move that would eventually be made – and undoubtedly contributed to the Führer's failure to make such a move at a time when it could have had so much greater effect. He still believed Dietrich would begin to make the necessary speed of progress, and that there was no need yet to reinforce von Manteuffel who seemed so have got off to a much better start.

17 DECEMBER

The German planners who remained awake during the first night of 'Wacht am Rhein' will have luxuriated in the glow of early success. If there were setbacks in the northern sector with Dietrich not gaining ground at the pace expected, elsewhere it was chiefly good news and, fundamentally from their point of view, the Americans had been caught unawares as intended and had proved unable to react quickly enough even to delay, let alone hold back, most of the assault units. Perhaps Hitler was right, maybe these brash additions to the Allied fighting strength really were to be found wanting when faced with a reversal of fortunes. But herein lay the fallibility of the German plan; its rigidity was based on the Führer's personal conviction that his scheme was right and no battlefield general could be trusted to make the right command decisions. Furthermore, without the flexibility needed in a mobile war zone, the military leaders on the ground were unable, with the exception of the mavericks like Peiper, to adjust to the conditions they encountered. If the messages coming down from the Führer said that the Americans would run, shocked and panicking from the field of battle, that must be the case.

The situation, of course, was quite the opposite. Eisenhower had been quick to employ an urgent but measured response. He had chosen to believe that this was a serious initiative on the part of the opposition and ordered the movement of support troops to the problem areas; he had not delayed in changing his priorities and his decision-making was to prove masterful throughout the next few weeks.

So the Germans had lulled themselves into a sense of false security concerning the absence of an Allied response. During the night many of the troops being sent to relieve or support the American forces at the front line had been on the move. General Bruce Clarke of Combat Command B had driven on ahead of his men and was in Bastogne before daybreak only to be promptly informed by Troy Middleton that, once his men had reached the area and after he had had some sleep, he was to hurry to St-Vith to assist Alan Jones and his beleaguered men stranded on the Schnee Eifel. The men from 7th Armored were making best speed to catch up with Clarke as they travelled south and were preceded on the same route by detachments from 1st Division. Due to arrive from the opposite direction were 10th Armored Division from Patton's Army, but they had not yet started.

Meanwhile, during the dark, cold night the Germans had put in hand one of the more daring elements of the operation. Colonel von der Heydte, a cousin of Count Felix von Stauffenburg, one of the July bomb plot conspirators, led the last German paratroop mission of the war with a five-company group from 6th Paratroop Regiment with instructions to land eight miles west of Monschau and prevent any American reinforcements from the north using the Eupen–

Malmédy road. The mission – Operation 'Stosser' (Hawk) – had already been delayed by 24 hours for the unbelievable reason that truck drivers due to ferry the paratroopers to the airfields could find neither the men nor the airfield by night! Nevertheless, the scheme showed that the German planners were alert to the fact that their incursions would draw a response from the Allies who would be most likely to bring down troops from the Aachen area.

Von der Heydte gave the mission only a ten per cent chance of success and the hapless truck drivers had not got it off to a good start, but worse was to come. He had already been prevented from using his own regiment, for the rather strange reason that its movement would alert the Allies, and was given a miscellaneous collection of inexperienced and sub-standard men from other groups. There needed to be observers on board the flights to control the operation, but there was no space available on the old, worn-out aircraft. Someone decided that the flight technicians should be left behind, so denying the pilots their most important crew member. Matters worsened when it was discovered that the troops had brought more weapons on board than had been allowed for with the result that one overloaded aircraft crashed on take-off and the others struggled to get airborne. Von der Heydte's men were not of the calibre he was used to, but recent recruits and dangerously inexperienced; only two had jumped on a live mission before.

THE RANGE OF GERMAN ADVANCES

The Ju 52 transport aircraft were obliged to fly low to avoid enemy radar and anti-aircraft fire, before climbing to ensure a safe drop in difficult terrain. Some

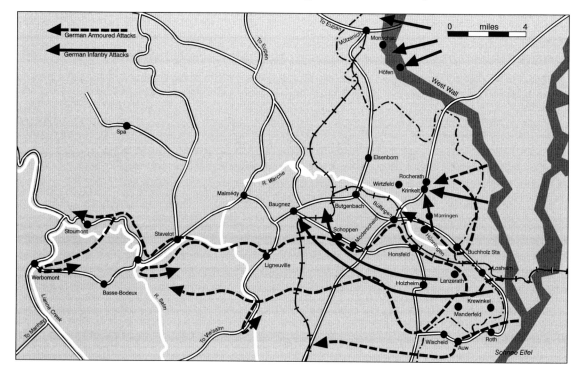

of the planes, now heavier and slower than usual, eventually reached their destination but not before the drop zone marker flares had burned out. Elsewhere, searchlights marking the route had not been turned on. As a result there was rampant confusion, faulty identification and inaccurate calls by the on-board observers, all of which meant that men were dropped as far afield as Bonn, fifty miles away, simply because lights were seen there, and others were released at the sighting of other flares that were also nothing to do with the mission. Such was the state of pandemonium that some of the young pilots, some flying this type of mission for the first time, forsook navigational data and started to fly north, away from the intended dropping area and into heavy ground fire that brought down several aircraft and their important cargoes.

Even that was not the end of problems in the air for this ill-fated mission. Despite extensive weather forecasting and reports from the dropping zone, winds in the area were much stronger than expected, and more than 100 who jumped were severely injured on landing and had to surrender. None of the radio sets dropped with the troops survived the fall. Von der Heydte reached the rendezvous with barely twenty men and, though they achieved their goal of sealing the road, their position proved unsustainable. Dietrich, who was supposed to have been in a position to join up with the paratroopers was still far from this point so within hours the order was given to disperse and make for home territory; a few made it but von der Heydte, wounded and ill, was forced to surrender near to Monschau. A final disaster befell two of the aircraft after the drop when they were chased and brought down over Germany by Allied night-fighters.

The Allies had been alerted to these flights just after midnight by an agent inside Germany. It had been clear that an airborne initiative was under way and, from the information obtained, its purpose could be foreseen. Undoubtedly the anti-aircraft fusillade that greeted the flight was prompted by this Intelligence, but it seems the Germans themselves did more than enough to ensure that the plan failed.

On the ground the pause in most German movement during the night had given more American troops the chance to escape the carnage at the Losheim Gap and head for Honsfeld and other less threatened locations. Before daybreak, however, the resourceful Jochen Peiper was also on the move and had driven west past Lanzerath to get close behind the withdrawing Americans. Soon the temporary refuge of Honsfeld would fall and Peiper would be eight miles on from the German border, but it was now that his independent nature got the better of him.

The young major, whose character failings were to become horribly apparent at Malmédy very soon, had the dream of crossing the Meuse very much in his mind. The Führer wanted him '... to, and over, the Meuse' and this dedicated supporter was determined to fulfil the directive. Already he was seriously short of fuel, and had personally witnessed some of the logistical nightmares beginning to afflict the campaign. including horse-drawn traffic holding up more vital traffic at an important river crossing north-west of Losheim. Just two miles to his north, but off the route he had been ordered to follow, lay Bullingen, where there was a large American fuel dump, but no German major had the authority, or the nerve, to break away from Hitler's own routing for the offensive, even if it meant taking possession of enough fuel to get him to the first main target and beyond. But Jochen Peiper was no ordinary German major.

Peiper diverted, using roads designated for use by 12th SS Panzer, fuelled up and promptly returned to his authorised route. This initiative, had it been discovered, could have meant instant court-martial, but it showed that need for flexibility which the entire operation lacked. Among the officers slavishly following orders over the coming days, and prejudicing the operation by so doing, there were undoubtedly men with the same resourcefulness of young Peiper but few had the nerve to show it.

Those American troops who had considered villages a few miles back from the front to be safe, or at least safer, had been quickly shown otherwise for Honsfeld and Bullingen were lost very early to the marauding Germans. Young soldiers stumbling over one another in a bid for sanctuary explained that they had had no alternative but to retreat and regroup, and it is entirely true that these defenders of the Losheim Gap had not been equipped to repel the numbers of infantry and armour that had flooded through the previous day. The Americans' situation north and south of the Gap was deteriorating by the hour, despite Dietrich's lack of progress, of which von Manteuffel wrote: 'Sepp Dietrich, totally disregarding his assignment, i.e., to thrust forward and aim for one mighty breakthrough, irrespective of what was happening to the right or left of the penetrating units – allowed himself to get bogged down in heavy fighting in the Elsenborn–Krinkelt area.'[6]

By daybreak the confusion among the troops at Honsfeld – some retreating, some moving forward, others preparing defences amidst the chaos – had brought about its downfall, with much loss of equipment, and further withdrawals. The chill morning of persistent mists and an all-over greyness saw Peiper's battle group now able to press on and leave a route to the west open for others. It was not a day when the Luftwaffe could venture forth in support and, more importantly, the Allied airmen would also have to remain on the ground.

It was becoming clear to divisional commanders that units considered to be strong and well-armed were already being compromised and all areas between them and the West Wall desperately needed strengthening, but with what? Farther back, corps commanders were beginning to get a clearer picture from the chaotic miscellany of phoned reports. V Corps HQ called off the attacking moves towards the Roer Dams being undertaken by elements of 2nd Division and ordered them to supplement the forces of the overrun 99th Division. Even so, as new moves were planned and orders given they were being rendered obsolete by further German advances. Major General Robertson, who had secured the decision to withdraw his attacking units, was interrupted in his issuing of new schemes as German armour was heard approaching his headquarters near Wirtsfeld, some ten miles from their starting-point a little more than 24 hours before.

Robertson set about redeploying his troops defensively, but even as he did so Dietrich's Volksgrenadiers and tanks had broken through the American lines farther north of the Losheim Gap and were moving round towards Rocherath and Krinkelt; from there they intended to move through the low downs of the Elsenborn Ridge and be well on their way to Spa, Verviers and the Meuse. This fact was already registering in the mind of Courtney Hodges some 24 miles from the front in Spa. He was not short of news from his beleaguered men, but now it was a question of deciding what his priorities should be, sifting the sad but irreparable cries for help from the strategically valid requests. He was aware by now that the offensive was of sufficient size and ambition to have made the Allied dispositions on this sector of the front quite inadequate. He knew of von der Heydte's mission but could not currently believe it to be of great substance. He knew that there were some pockets of resistance, and that Dietrich was at the head of the northern flank of the German push; it was clear to him that the German intention was to regain territory, certainly take away some of the Allied initiative, perhaps drive the Allies right back to the Meuse, and – he scarcely dared think of it – push for the Channel ports again.

Hodges became concerned chiefly with the northern flank of the German breakthrough for if these troops were at Bullingen and Krinkelt, and paratroops were being dropped west of Monschau, the aim of von Rundstedt, for Allied commanders were still believing the senior German field marshal to be at the core of the plan, would be to take the shortest route to the sea. He needed to stem the flood at a point where he could hold some advantage and stand a chance of retaining it. His maps suggested the Elsenborn Ridge was the place for this because, if he could get men and armour there and above the marauding German forces, he stood a chance of holding the forward drive until new tactics could be devised. He called Omar Bradley at Versailles with the desperate plea for the two airborne divisions that he knew were held in reserve. This modest man had fought in this area in 1917–18, and won the Distinguished Service Cross for his efforts. He was a low-key character who got things done, a man who, when he pressed the 'Urgent' button, could be trusted to have responded correctly to the given situation. He was being brought to military prominence by this sudden German initiative, but for the moment, he only got Bradley to agree to pass his request to Eisenhower.

The latter was already sure that the German moves had presented him with a command problem. Their initiative had split Bradley's army group and, positioned at Luxembourg, he was not well situated to lead his two northern armies.

The resolution to this was probably clear to Eisenhower, but it would require great tact on his part to get it past his American colleagues.

If Hodges knew his men due east were in trouble, there was also no doubting that those of 106th Division facing the onslaught from von Manteuffel's Fifth Army on and around the Schnee Eifel were under equal pressure. General Alan Jones was expecting 7th Armored Division to arrive in support and had very few of his own men to use now that he had all but lost two regiments on the hills around which the Germans had driven their pincer movement. He wanted the reinforcements of the 7th to stem the flow at Schönberg, just six miles from his command post in a church school house in St-Vith, but until they arrived he sent what men he had to meet the approaching Volksgrenadiers and delay them as long as possible.

Jones' mood was shortly to be raised and lowered in the moment it took for General Bruce Clarke to walk into the St-Vith HQ and announce that the relieving force consisted of him and a driver, they having come on ahead of his troops for whom he could not give an accurate arrival time. Clarke had had no idea how desperate the situation was.

Not letting his depression get the better of him, Jones set about getting an air drop to his stranded men (who included his son) on the Schnee Eifel, who were surely short of food, medical supplies and ammunition. He got an assurance that such items would be parachuted in immediately and radioed the two regiments with the news, though, as it turned out, the pilots to fly the mission would not be given their instructions until the following morning. Thinking he had organised immediate if temporary respite for his men, Jones next considered how he could protect his own position which would certainly be under threat shortly if the last few men he had sent forward that morning could not stop the Germans. Just as Jones and Clarke had begun to discuss the options news came through that the token force he had sent out just a few hours before had already been forced to retreat and were only a mile outside the town. This news arrived just as the Generals had been joined by a distraught Colonel Devine who had lost most of his 14th Cavalry Group and withdrawn to the edge of the town.

Some American heavy armour had been directed to a German advance north of the town, with the result that the lead tank was knocked out and the static column was shot-up until it chose to retreat and reassemble. It was a rare moment of American success in a very bad morning on the Ardennes front. For every man who was remaining calm a hundred were racing away from the front, some under orders to do so, others in small groups or singly who had determined to flee to safety and fight another day.

It was barely half-way through the second day of 'Wacht am Rhein' and some of the fiercest action had been seen towards the southern sector where von Manteuffel's main task was to reach and take the crucial town of Bastogne as soon as possible. The first strategic obstacle in the path of his men would be the picturesque Luxembourg town of Clervaux, just six miles west of Dasburg where they had broken out of their West Wall defences; the town must be taken by noon and it was up to units of Kampfgruppe Peiper to make sure of this.

The town and its ancient castle lay at the end of a narrow and sometimes precipitous winding road down from the mountains west of the Our valley. It was not conducive to a rapid advance, but Colonel Fuller, whose command post for his 110th Regiment was in the town's Claravallis Hotel, knew the Germans were coming and since early morning was aware they were within firing range of the castle.

Although this was indeed the case, von Manteuffel had not got his men and tanks across the Our as quickly as he had planned and, though the Dasburg bridge had been fully used, the crossing at Gemund, six miles farther south, had become snarled up by slow-moving horse-drawn wagons of ammunition and other supplies. It was one of hundreds of examples of the logistics of the campaign being found wanting; in this case the delay had been caused by the Russian

Left: A heavily armed Panzergrenadier carries ammunition boxes forward.

personnel manning the horses not understanding German or being prepared to operate at the pace demanded by the increasingly irate commanders and tank crews.

Fuller knew nothing of this; he only knew that he had too few troops and armour to defend Clervaux and he understood the consequences of its fall. The town of Marnach, half-way from Dasburg, housed a garrison but this was over-run by mid-morning and Fuller's calls for extra help had apparently fallen on deaf ears. Heinerscheid, four miles to the north, was sent five Shermans to help stem the German onslaught, but all around him the General's defensive outposts were being taken. None of the Shermans got to Heinerscheid and, in the south-ern sector, the attack from Gemund had accounted for American strong-points at Hosingen, Weiler, Holtsthum and even Consthum, the latter a full seven miles from the border and less than six from the important town of Wiltz.

By midday Fuller was making another call for extra armour. Speaking to General Cota in Wiltz, Fuller was able to report the sighting of twelve Tiger tanks positioned above the town ready to press home the next decisive push; Cota could only offer some self-propelled guns – no match for the giant Tigers.

A few hours later Clervaux was all but encircled. American armour in the streets close to Fuller's Command Post was being destroyed before his eyes. When the extra guns arrived from Wiltz they were immediately despatched against the Tigers but were quickly forced to withdraw from the unequal fight. Munshausen and Urspelt, respectively to the south and north of Clervaux, were lost by 1600 and, though Fuller was doing his very best to obey the order to hold his positions at all costs, Clervaux had already been effectively cut off by von Manteuffel's faster moves to the north and the south; by dusk there was no pur-pose in standing to fight as Tiger tanks were in the street below his own HQ. As he sought permission from Wiltz to withdraw, and heard the request refused, the hotel was shaken by the fire of increasing numbers of German tanks and power was lost. In the darkness someone found a rear exit from the building and Fuller, with a motley collection of staff, retreating soldiers, injured officers and sundry locals, made for it and evaded capture clambering across a narrow iron bridge which led to the hills behind.

Colonel Fuller had done all he could to hold Clervaux, but his most trenchant pleas to his men and his astute management of the resources at his disposal had counted for nothing when faced with the fierce German advance. The actions being taken behind the scenes had been insufficient in this corner of the Allied Front.

When a rapid advance is planned through a defensive line it will, if successful in breaking through and choosing to continue, surely encounter reinforce-ments being called forward to support the defenders. Such was going to be the case in the Ardennes, and both combatants knew it. While the days were still overcast there was a limit to what the Allied commanders could do but send units by road and hope they would arrive in time. It was hope indeed that drove many of the Allied decisions in these first two days because no one yet knew the extent of the German ambitions nor therefore how far they intended to push forward, what support forces would be following the main thrust and even whether Hitler now really did have the major new weaponry he had been threatening to unleash. The Allied command was only now beginning to come to terms with the fact that their Intelligence people had let them down, that the enemy *did* have men and machinery, and the will, to fight back, and had not simply been building up the West Wall defences as they had convinced themselves was the case.

It is no surprise that Jochen Peiper was in the vanguard of the German advance. Just as Patton had been known to move too quickly and out of kilter with neighbouring divisions, so the young German officer was relishing the chance to move forward at speed and he had little regard for anything other than his own men and their next target. By early afternoon on 17 December, he was heading for Baugnez, some seven miles on from his unauthorised refuelling stop of the day before, and was now confident that he had broken through the American resistance. He had driven towards Bullingen but turned sharply left to head in the direction of Moderscheid, Schoppen and Baugnez.

This particular move had puzzled the Americans for those around the base of the Elsenborn Ridge had not completed their defensive lines and knew themselves still susceptible to attack. Had the Germans moved against them here on this second day of their advance they could have trapped both the 99th and 2nd Divisions; they were unaware that only his determination to keep to good roads that would hasten his movement had caused Peiper to use the Bullingen road at all.

During the afternoon it was Hunningen, two miles south-east of Bullingen, that was the focus of German attention in this area. Because some breaks in the cloud had seen Allied fighters active, the attack on Hunningen had been held back, but now a heavy artillery barrage was followed by massed infantry attacking from south-east of the town. A show of resourcefulness, when an American observer in a church spire used his advantageous position to direct withering fire into the advancing lines, and further accurate automatic fire from foxholes, stalled wave after wave of German rushes and even an order to withdraw was ignored by these 1st Battalion units under Colonel Hightower who felt he would put his men at greater risk by moving back than by staying and fighting until reinforcements arrived. The Americans held their positions until the close of the day.

The Germans were also trying the attain the higher ground of Elsenborn via the twin villages of Krinkelt and Rocherath, a couple of miles north of Bullingen. The artillery bombardment of the first morning had certainly given the attackers the advantage, but they soon suffered losses and capture in fights with 3rd Battalion, 395th Infantry forces, yet still got some men through the spaces between the 3rd and 1st Battalions. The 1st had been badly pummelled from the outset and, though their mortar and machine-gun fire was accurate and sustained, parts of their defences were virtually surrounded in the first two hours. But they managed to redeploy and had severely dented the enemy's drive before the end of the first day.

Once extra German forces had been brought to bear, the brave resistance in front of Rocherath and Krinkelt began to wilt. Tanks and infantry overran the foxholes and such was the ferocity of the assault that company after company was prevented from withdrawing and attempts to block the gaps proved futile. Such withdrawal as was achieved was modest and by nightfall on 17 December, 1st Battalion had been reduced to just over 200 men.

Earlier in the day the 7th Division's Combat Command Reserve had been weaving its meandering route south to St-Vith to join up with General Jones' 106th Division; it had reached Malmédy, some eleven miles as the crow flies from Jones but more like twenty miles by the winding roads of the region. If they were able to maintain their smooth, unfettered progress they would soon be at Baugnez.

Ahead of the CCR on the uphill road from Malmédy was a small convoy of jeeps and trucks making up B Battery of the 285th Field Artillery Observation Battalion. This unit was a minor element of the American forces, but its men were about to feature in an incident that would galvanise many a hesitant American heart in the coming days.

At this juncture Peiper's men were on higher ground than the Americans and spotted them first. They opened fire until Peiper stopped them. Such firepower wasn't necessary at this point and the observation convoy was quickly captured and brought back to Madame Adèle Bodarwe's cafe at the Baugnez crossroads where they were herded into a small field. What happened then is not altogether clear, but it seems that a revolver shot at the prisoners from either a trigger-happy guard or a passing German armoured vehicle, induced mayhem that saw the entire group riddled by machine-guns and pistols. The full group of hapless captives fell where they stood, some dead, all others wounded. Even then, other German soldiers walked among the prostrate forms, shooting again if they saw any sign of life. It was remarkable that any survived – eighty-six did not – but when calm returned the few still breathing were able to whisper plans for an escape. Eventually, twenty rose uncertainly and tried to run or crawl to a wood a few hundred yards away. They were noticed and again rifle shots rang out. Just three made it to the wood, did what they could to dress their own wounds and stumbled off to the west, eventually arriving at Malmédy. Kampfgruppe Peiper were again the culprits when nineteen unarmed Americans were shot down at Honsfeld and fifty at Bullingen.[7] Although it cannot be said that Peiper himself squeezed the trigger on these occasions, or was even present, the massacre shows clearly the type of men he had under command, as was recognised by post-war trials. Researchers have it that Peiper's men killed close to 350 American prisoners and at least 100 Belgian civilians at a dozen locations during their advance.

Peiper had a reputation for brutality when he was commanding a battalion in Russia and it was from that theatre that many of his Ardennes group came. It was a recipe for disaster when combined with his determination to move at the pace ordered by his Führer, but the Malmédy incident put steel into American spines, and the eventual reversal of his fortunes in the Ardennes was all the more satisfying.

Peiper's group were now heading for Ligneuville, to the south, which 7th Division's CCR were passing quietly through on their long drive from the north. Captain Green, whose men of Combat Command B of 9th Armored Division were stationed around the town, had watched the 7th Division's units pass by but held his position, as instructed, to meet other supply convoys as they came through. Although there was occasional distant rumbling of heavy guns neither Green nor his men, nor the local inhabitants, imagined any likelihood of their peaceful sojourn being broken – until, that is, an engineer drove a bulldozer at breakneck speed into the town centre calling to Green that he had been shot at and that enemy tanks were just a few hundred yards away.

Green ordered his men to prepare to move out, and had a jeep take him to investigate. After a minute or so he got out and walked on alone, but rounding a bend came face to face with Peiper's column and was promptly ordered to stand to one side as the vehicles passed him. While thinking that his troops had nothing adequate to oppose this group, the lead vehicle of the convoy burst into flames, zigzagged across the road and brought the column to a halt and open to the fire of a sole Sherman tank firing from the town centre.

It was a short-lived effort. One of Peiper's guns soon found the Sherman and put it out of action with a single round. Now the column was able to press on through the town in the wake of the last of Green's retreating troops, and send advance units on towards the River Amblève *en route* for Stavelot, a further seven miles away, by an unmade road.

A few miles to the south, the situation at St-Vith had not improved. It was surely at the mercy of the approaching German forces unless and until CCB arrived to join General Clarke, but they had become snarled up in a huge log-jam of vehicles on the main road from Vielsalm that no one seemed able to dislodge. Because of the sheer weight of traffic and the collision of retreating vehicles and those heading for the front, Clarke's forces would not get clear until mid-afternoon, and the General, who had assumed sole control of the defence of the town from the dispirited and flagging General Jones, was in a black mood. How was he supposed to defend the place?

It was beginning to get dark before the relieving forces arrived on the outskirts of the town and this only after Clarke himself had cleared the roads of senior officers retreating from the area. The first column of tanks he diverted to the Schönberg road with orders to link up with the small group of battling engineers. They would soon claim their first Panther and cause one group of enemy vehicles to beat a hasty retreat, but this was a small gain in a situation that remained dire. St-Vith was almost cut off from the road to the north and nearly so in the south. It was no longer the minor territory of the Schnee Eifel that held a pocket of Allied troops but a huge swathe of land from there to St-Vith was now under threat. If the town fell Hitler's offensive would have gained a major foothold by the second day of the operation.

If the Americans were sombre and wary, it might have been expected that the German commanders would be in buoyant mood, but this was not so. Both von Manteuffel and Dietrich had their orders and knew their progress to date was not sufficient to satisfy the Führer or, for that matter, Field Marshal Model who was on the battlefield.

LXVI CORPS ATTACK, 16–19 DECEMBER

Dietrich was beginning to become embarrassed by the almost reckless pace of Peiper's advance for it was setting a precedent that he and others had not achieved. While the young cavalier was past Ligneuville and heading for Stavelot, 12th SS Panzer was still delayed at Krinkelt and Rocherath, and the remainder of

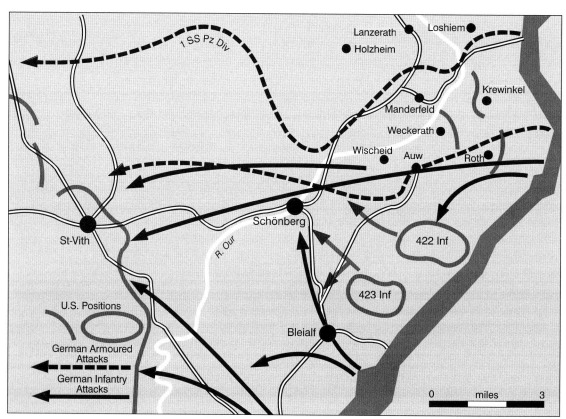

Peiper's 1st SS Panzers were also well behind the units he was leading. At his evening briefing Dietrich demanded a better performance on the third day, though he was probably unable to say how this could be achieved, and Skorzeny, whose Operation 'Greif' could not be started until more progress was made, proposed that his specialist troops be used for standard combat requirements in order to accelerate matters.

Von Manteuffel was staying overnight in Schönberg, tantalisingly close to St-Vith but not that much farther forward than Dietrich at Manderfeld. His main concern was that his troops attacking through the northern sector of his command area had been having a struggle. He had needed St-Vith, for its control of the road network in the area and for its access to the railway, and in a chance meeting with Model the senior man allocated the Führer's Escort Brigade, currently held in reserve, to speed-up progress next day. The two men must have been desperate for Dietrich to get his forces moving, for it would be of little value if only Jochen Peiper and a handful of troops were on schedule and advanced too far ahead of their support units; and there were no other teams moving alongside the young trail-blazer.

It was already clear that the best chance of German success lay in a revision of the plan; Dietrich's men should be diverted south in support of von Manteuffel's swifter progress, but Dietrich was not likely to find the idea appealing, Model seemed unwilling or unable to enforce the move, and all realised that to change the Führer's grand scheme would not be easy to accomplish.

The evening saw mixed fortunes for the Americans with units of 1st Division managing to dig in at Butgenbach on the Elsenborn Ridge just before German forces arrived there, but elsewhere stragglers retreating from the débâcle endured by 99th Division were unwittingly obstructing other attempts to create Hodges' defensive lines on the Ridge. The Americans' difficulties were alleviated by the Germans' own disorganisation and piecemeal attacking around Krinkelt and Rocherath. On the eastern edge of adjacent Rocherath, an American roadblock was destroyed by three German tanks before more armour following them was mined and fired on, causing great confusion and temporary withdrawal. When the enemy tried again, the newly placed artillery on the Ridge above the scene again forced some of the tanks to retreat though others continued through to the town, accompanied by a large infantry force. There was, indeed, rampant confusion in the fields and villages below Elsenborn, most of it among the Allied troops who were poorly placed to stave off the Germans who were under great pressure to move on from this area before the third day of 'Wacht am Rhein'.

If the first day of the offensive had come as a shock to the Allies, the second was no less shocking and the implications hit the most senior command centres in Luxembourg, Spa and Versailles – the Germans were going to take some stopping. The American forces had not witnessed the 'Blitzkrieg' tactics of 1940, but they imagined they were experiencing something very similar now.

18 DECEMBER

Forty-eight hours into his campaign, Adolf Hitler will have looked at the reports from the front with mixed emotions. He had undoubtedly caught the enemy by surprise, and to a degree even he could have barely thought possible, and one of his military stars, Jochen Peiper, had driven far into opposition territory, dozens of miles further than many other units including some from the Kampfgruppe bearing his name. But Hitler's futile bravado in proclaiming that his troops would see the Meuse in two days was now seen to be as foolish as von Rundstedt had always claimed. Little ground had been gained, opposition defences had not collapsed and the almost perfect logistics that had got the attacking forces into position were now deserting them as supply roads became clogged with tanks and trucks, the latter often carrying loads of little consequence holding up the former that had been due to press the attacks forward.

The Führer will have noted that another of his celebrated warriors, Otto Skorzeny, had seen his participation almost stillborn, at least in respect of the main aim of his mission, and the dramatic parachute drop behind enemy lines by von der Heydte had been a disaster. Furthermore, the fact that Peiper could report personal achievement counted for nothing if it was an isolated case, and to be as far ahead of the other groups as he was carried more risk than benefit.

The Führer must have also been close to accepting that his beloved Sepp Dietrich had not performed well. Operating on the inner curve of the attack route, he had been first hindered, then delayed and later utterly stalled by a combination of attacks by 2nd Division and the inadequate back-up of men and *matériel*. The Reich loyalist and Hitler favourite was proving many doubters right; his battlefield planning and resolution was found wanting. Where Model, and even von Manteuffel, were good managers of a battle-zone, the butcher from Hawagen was a poor replacement for the senior commanders Hitler could have chosen for this role had the July bomb plot not caused him to mistrust so many of them.

The Americans had noticed Peiper's dramatic gains. Courtney Hodges concluded that if Peiper could move as fast as he had, surely it was intended that others should do so too; and if and when his own forward defensive lines were pierced elsewhere he would be facing advances of similar pace. None of his replenishing forces were going to arrive in time to stop the young German, however, and he was situated above Stavelot as another opaque grey sky greeted all combatants on this third day. Hodges was setting great store on the arrival of 82 Airborne and the 9th and 30th Divisions from the north, to prevent the vanguard of the German drive curving right towards Holland. Peiper's lead vehicles were now only eight or so miles from his First Army HQ, and the permanent residents of Spa were beginning to panic even if the phlegmatic American General was not – at least not yet.

In the French capital and at SHAEF HQ in nearby Versailles there were mixed reactions to the overnight news. Parisians and leaders of their Army were fretful, desperate for more news and American reassurance; Eisenhower, by comparison, was calm but urgent in his planning and decision-making. He knew now that he had been right in his initial judgement that the German moves were a full offensive designed to take and keep ground, though he could only guess at the ultimate aim. He also knew now that substantial changes of plan and a significant redeployment of forces was called for. He resolved to abandon Patton's imminent moves on the Saar, have him move north and hit the German drive from the side, and he set up a meeting with Bradley and Patton for the following day. The change of task for Patton would be a most astute move and would have crucial ramifications.

It was not in the nature of Jochen Peiper to rest on his laurels or, for that matter, consider the wisdom of his rapid advance in comparison with other units. He was set on meeting his own personal remit of crossing the Meuse and heading for Antwerp, irrespective of the consequences of such unbridled haste. His first task of the morning was to cross the Amblève into Stavelot, and he expected to ride roughshod over any defence encountered.

His first obstacle was a narrow stone bridge. If he could cross before the American forces could blow it his job was half done. Fire from one of his Tiger tanks accounted for two tank destroyers manoeuvring to fire at his column and an order for his Tigers and Panthers to race for the bridge caused American infantry to hurry back to the shelter of the town. The bridge was not mined, the tanks crossed and came under bazooka fire on the other side. Although this accounted for three of Peiper's vehicles, his prompt diversion of most of his force around the point of fire, leaving a smaller unit to wipe out the defenders, meant that he was through Stavelot and on the way to his next objective – the village of Trois Ponts – with relatively little delay.

If he could get through Trois Ponts, Peiper reckoned his route to the Meuse could be unhindered and he would meet the demands of his Führer. The American troops in the town knew only that they must destroy the main bridges across the river before the Germans arrived. Although they had made a start, and positioned a 57mm anti-tank gun near the underpass the enemy would have to use, they had begun the job too late; Peiper saw what they were up to and promptly ordered the attack.

A direct hit halted the leading tank of Peiper's convoy. Now began a race against time. Could this minor artillery piece hold off a score of tanks until the bridge was detonated? It did so for almost fifteen minutes while the German tank crews tried to spot it. In the nick of time the bridge over the Amblève shook to the sound of mighty explosions that left an irreparable hole in its centre rendering it unusable. Peiper screamed with rage and ordered his tanks forward. They soon located the lone gun and destroyed it and its crew, but the young commander knew that his preferred route to the west, through Basse-Bodeux, was now unusable. He quickly decided to make a detour along a narrower, undulating road to the north which, he estimated, would mean a delay but perhaps of only an hour or two.

Although separated by hills, Peiper was already only a few miles due south of US First Army HQ at Spa, and the sound of his advance could just be heard. Courtney Hodges, based in the historic Hotel Britannica there, was already being urged to withdraw from the town to a safer area; it was advice he was disinclined to take though later in the day he would allow most of his staff to leave before gathering his own papers and effects and joining them. At this juncture he didn't know that Peiper, still far ahead of any other German unit, had no interest in Spa and was solely focused on the Meuse which he would reach, in the first instance, by threading his way through the valleys to the north-west of his current position. This day would end with his unit having advanced some fifteen miles despite the delay at Stavelot and a late attack by fighter-bombers that had taken out ten of his armoured vehicles.

The German troops involved in the proposed advance between the Honsfelderwald and the Elsenborn Ridge surely knew by now that they were under-performing. Their intended route to Antwerp – and to the Meuse – was the shortest, but they were stalled, and still not past their first modest geograph-

Below: The massacre of US troops at Malmédy.

ical hurdle. The bloodied American defenders were seeking to get 2nd and 99th Divisions back to the comparative safety of the Elsenborn Ridge while re-forming other groups to hold Wirtzfeld and, for as long as they could, Krinkelt and Rocherath. Onslaughts from German tanks and infantry were skilfully repulsed throughout the night, and although some German units eventually reached the outskirts of the villages, the delay had enabled the next line of defence, at Wirtzfeld, to be properly prepared.

Just before light on this third day the Germans mounted fresh attacks on Rocherath. Enveloping fog made the American artillery on Elsenborn less effective than it might have been, and the contest became an infantry battle along the foxhole line. Bayonets and knives came into play, and bazookas accounted for a few German tanks. One assault after another wore the defenders down and one American company after another was lost. Eventually German tanks got into the town and the close-quarter fighting became fiercer yet; buildings were taken and reoccupied several times, with American Shermans managing to account for some German armour.

Simultaneously Krinkelt was being fought over, troops of both sides seldom knowing how their fellows were faring just a few hundred yards away. American shellfire regularly delayed waves of German advances here, though a few tanks did get as far as the road to Wirtzfeld before suffering at the hands of American tanks, tank destroyers and bazooka units. In a very confused situation at the end of the day, the twin villages were still in Allied hands and the German advance in this sector was still lagging far behind others.

Elsewhere on the morning of 18 December, German progress continued to fail to match Peiper's manic pace. Where defence had been routed or by-passed, the Allies resorted to spoiling tactics wherever they could, driven to last stands, ambushes and crude counter-attacks by demands from senior men behind the front. The leaden skies were still forbidding worthwhile Allied air action and damaged or poorly manned communications systems failed to get messages around the battle front. Supplies by air seldom got through and were sometimes misdirected. So confused was the battle-zone, especially around the Schnee Eifel, that Allied troops were often retreating into the path of German groups that had passed around or through them.

Had von Manteuffel forced small advance columns of his tank divisions to move ahead of the main groups, as Peiper seemed to be doing of his own volition, he might have reached St-Vith and Bastogne by the morning of 18 December, but this had not been his policy; he was still short of each town although making good progress in his own estimation. He still had to tackle Wiltz, a little more than ten miles from his start-point and about the same again east of Bastogne. Farther north other Panzer Lehr teams were pursuing another route via Drauffelt and Eschweiller, and north again, having by-passed Clervaux, his 2nd Panzer Division was homing in on the strategic town from the north-east.

The vital factor was that these German forces must get to Bastogne before the Americans could bring in fresh troops to defend it. Both sides knew that their opponents considered the town to be a vital possession.

With Eisenhower having released the 82nd and 101st Airborne Divisions, the commanders confronting the German onslaught continued their efforts to delay, confound and disrupt the enemy until such time that the skies cleared or fresh ground forces arrived. This meant that, even though the 101st were heading for the town – the 82nd were diverted by Hodges to tackle Peiper's astonishing forward thrust – other reinforcements had to be found and deployed. Combat Command B of 10th Armored Division, commanded by Colonel William Roberts, was withdrawn from action near the city of Luxembourg and ordered to drive the thirty miles north to threatened Bastogne. On Roberts' appearance in mid-afternoon, General Middleton ordered that his men, once they arrived, should be despatched in three task forces to reinforce the modest defensive barrier already being organised to the east of the town. Shortly afterwards he was briefing Brigadier General McAuliffe who had travelled ahead of his 101st Airborne men to meet Middleton.

The first two of the task forces formed from Roberts' men were moved out as they arrived and soon the road from Wiltz was in the care of Lieutenant Colonel James O'Hara with thirty tanks and 500 men, and a similar group was sent down the road from Mageret and Longvilly and was put under command of Lieutenant Colonel Henry Cherry. These groups knew exactly what they were being sent to do, though they were still unsure about what the Germans were going to be able to throw at them when they arrived.

Perhaps because of their rush to get into position or because, having got there, they were busy strengthening their defences, a third group, Task Force Harper, was unprepared for the barrage of tank fire that hit it soon after dark. The tanks that were able to engage were quickly knocked out and some of the scattering infantry mown down before the remainder beat a speedy retreat to Longvilly. But their attackers intended to approach Bastogne from the north-east, via Noville, the very town where Middleton planned to use Roberts' third task force.

At Longvilly the stragglers joined up with an already patchwork group under the command of Colonel Gilbreth. He had taken on men retreating from his own roadblocks and from even closer to the German border and was now destined to face divisions of Volksgrenadier and Panzer Lehr forces approaching from Oberwach.

Back in Bastogne confusion reigned: the inhabitants were panicking; the back-up forces had arrived; retreating soldiers who had sought the safety of the town brought in their wounded and told tales of massive tanks in huge numbers and great loss of life. Understandably there was tension at senior level, and a dispute between Brigadier General Anthony McAuliffe and Roberts as to who should command was only settled by Middleton insisting that their working together was essential to the future of Bastogne. Roberts, hating to use his men so disparately, sent his third task force, under William Desobry, towards Noville and hoped that his outposts and roadblocks would still be intact in the morning, though what he probably prayed for was an end to the wretched fog, low cloud and cold.

The corps commander of the three divisions homing in on Bastogne was General Heinrich von Lüttwitz, another First World War veteran with great experience of armoured warfare. He was a solid, determined soldier with a passion for achieving his goals that saw him able to inspire his troops despite the appearance – rotund, paternal, and wearing a monocle – of a provincial bank manager. Aware, thanks to the insecurity of US radio traffic, that Eisenhower had ordered up additional troops, he wanted his men in the town first. Although he was behind schedule, he was confident Bastogne would be his by the following day, the 19th.

By late evening, Major General Fritz Bayerlein, commander of Panzer Lehr Division, was six miles to the east of Bastogne and desperate to get there. Von Lüttwitz expected him to arrive that night, but progress had been slow over increasingly muddied and crowded roads. In also desperation he gambled on a more direct route which, according to his map, was good enough to get him to Mageret and then on to Bastogne. It soon proved to be a critical error for after a mile or so, his vehicles were becoming bogged down in mud that bid fair to get worse. He persevered, but was to rue this error of judgement.

Although German progress towards Bastogne was proving troublesome, the Allies were not faring too well either. A convoy of 11,000 men of the 101st in some 400 trucks was rattling along with full headlights, but between them and Bastogne a still, dense fog was delaying their commander, Major General Matthew Ridgway, from getting to the town ahead of them so as to begin the meeting that would determine the nature of their deployment.

Like almost everyone in the Ardennes, Ridgway was still relatively ignorant of the situation, save that apparently the Germans were in the ascendant. Many of the Allied officers still had no idea of the state of play to their north or south, and some of them, especially around the Elsenborn Ridge, didn't know whether they were supposed to be attacking or defending, which direction they should move in, and whether the next group they encountered would be friend or foe.

On the night of 18 December 1st SS Panzer units gathered in Bullingen in preparation for a morning assault on Butgenbach, three miles up the river valley to the north-west. Simultaneously the forward command post of 12th SS Panzer was being set up alongside them and a battalion of 25th SS Panzer Grenadier Regiment with tanks had also arrived; still more diverse groups were to arrive in the next few hours to make this one of the largest concentrations of German forces during the Ardennes battle. The tanks had turned the area into a mass of mud which remained unfrozen during the night. The assault early next morning was thwarted by the slowness of the tank movement and the accuracy of the high-explosive rained upon them by 33rd Field Artillery Battalion. It would be mid-morning before the attackers would try again.

As 18 December came to a close German radio was announcing collapsing Allied defences. The calm pronouncements from Brussels, Paris, London and the USA did little to stem the waves of concern and even panic.

At Hitler's headquarters the veteran von Rundstedt had retained the doom-laden attitude he had had from the start. He was still pressing for total abandonment of the enterprise and the setting up of fresh defences around the territory they had secured; he argued that St-Vith was still in American hands, as was Bastogne and, because of the weather and Allied resistance, the essential speed of advance had not been as good as had been expected

It is fair to say that Model, at this point, was showing more confidence and urging Hitler to divert more forces to von Manteuffel so as to complete the full breakthrough, albeit on a revised route. He probably knew, however, that Hitler was desperate to keep his SS Panzer Division separate from the Army command structure, and Dietrich was his man.

GERMAN MOVES ACROSS THE RIVER OUR

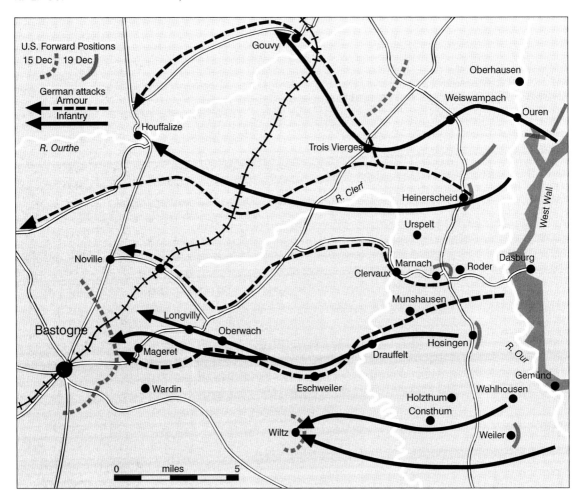

19 DECEMBER

At the start of the fourth day of the offensive, a most unlikely yet significant circumstance was occurring. We have identified that Bayerlein's approach to Bastogne was being hindered by his own gamble in taking his fifteen tanks plus half-tracks and other vehicles carrying four companies of men down unmade roads, but he was no timid greenhorn making great decisions for the first time. A veteran of the Eastern Front and the Desert Campaign, and a tough, uncompromising officer, he had learned much from the likes of Guderian and Rommel. One would not expect such a man to be uncertain in his situation; surely it was opportune that his experience was at the helm in the capture of Bastogne.

Because of the misreading of his map, or rather his reluctance to take a safe but slower route, the General had not reached Mageret until the early hours of the morning. Although tired and frustrated, his men quickly captured an American medical team after a brief fire fight, and began questioning the locals about the disposition of American troops in the area. One Belgian citizen told Bayerlein that he had seen a group of fifty tanks, led by a major general, heading towards Longvilly just hours before. Although this information was inaccurate – the man had seen Task Force Cherry, which had only thirty tanks – the German general seemed disconcerted by the news and thought perhaps that he might had been cut off thanks to the unexpected route he had taken. He could hear firing in the distance, and became confused.

He delayed for three hours before deciding to move on towards Bastogne, but then his lead tank hit a mine and, his column moving ever slower now, he was still three miles short of Bastogne centre when dawn broke through the same dulling low grey cloud of the last few days. Visibility was minimal and this contributed to the General's unease. Any field commander needs to be able to see his objective, send out scouts and literally see his next step. He had met no substantial opposition though he knew that lay ahead of him, and believed erroneously that American units were behind him. He waited again.

While he could and should have continued to advance, Bayerlein was right about there being American defenders in his path. While he waited for better natural light, General McAuliffe was despatching Colonel Julian Ewell and a poorly equipped 1st Battalion of the 501st Parachute Regiment directly towards the spot where Bayerlein was stalled. Ewell and his men passed various withdrawing American units and were then suddenly stopped by machine-gun fire. Ewell assumed that it was a German roadblock and promptly dispersed his men, but he had walked straight into Bayerlein and was facing firepower he had no chance of matching.

If Ewell was confused, Bayerlein quickly exhibited the characteristics of a rabbit caught in headlights. He too thought that he was facing a heavy armoured group and felt it reckless to try to fight his way through, so he set himself new priorities: turn his column round, attack the Americans he was sure were behind him on the Longvilly road and then turn again to attack Bastogne. Shortly after midday he was at the outskirts of Longvilly and had located a line of static enemy vehicles heading in the direction of Mageret, but unknown to him the 26th Volksgrenadier Division was about to mount an attack on the same group from the south-east. The resulting storm of fire power persuaded units from 2nd Panzer by-passing the town to the north to join in too. Task Force Cherry, still positioned a little to the west, could not prevent the ensuing carnage but fought stoutly enough to induce some caution among the German command.

It was a massacre, but out of the wretchedness came remarkable benefit. For all the loss of life, the wrecking or capturing of two hundred vehicles, and the temporary renewal of confidence among the Germans, Bayerlein's indecision and now the brave delaying action by Lieutenant Colonel Henry Cherry and his men, meant that the Germans could not begin their offensive against Bastogne until a full day later than they might have done. It was a major factor in the whole campaign as we shall see when we see how close Bastogne came to being taken.

The American losses east of Bastogne were nothing in comparison with the situation in the area of the Schnee Eifel on this fourth day. Model was urging von Manteuffel to capture the strategic centre of St-Vith and thus match the momentum achieved by Peiper and, they assumed, Bayerlein and von Lüttwitz, but valuable artillery for this particular attack was being delayed by Dietrich using roads that were not earmarked for his men; the result was a traffic jam of epic proportions and Model himself had to take charge of making a path through for the essential fire power.

Despite this poor German performance and sturdy American defence, overwhelming strength in numbers and equipment would take its toll and, on this day, men from Schönberg to Krinkelt and Rocherath would find themselves retreating or surrendering.

Some men of George Descheneaux's 422nd Regiment of the 106th Division were forced to surrender after a futile assault on Schönberg, and Charles Cavender's regiment was also in poor shape made no better by an instance of 'friendly fire' when nervous units of the 422nd fired on his 2nd Battalion. The failure to drop supplies to the American forces in the Schnee Eifel was leaving the men there with nothing to put in their stomachs or their armour.

By mid-afternoon the American forces effectively imprisoned within the woods around Schönberg numbered almost 10,000 and though more of Descheneaux's men were tantalisingly close to the town they too were outnumbered and overpowered by a Panzer brigade. Enemy firepower was cutting men to shreds and at all points of the compass the depressing decision to surrender was being argued, there being as many wanting to fight on as those who saw the white flag as the only option. In the event, upwards of 8,000 men were captured and, as a result, the Germans believed that they could now concentrate on St-Vith.

Even on the Elsenborn Ridge, Hodges' chosen location for countering the Germans' northern advance, the day saw frantic efforts to improvise obstacles, but by nightfall the order to withdraw reached the exhausted soldiers.

If the Germans were well behind the schedule set by Hitler, they were through at many points where their commanders might have expected stiff resistance and further delays.

Earlier in the day Eisenhower had met Bradley, Patton and others at Verdun. The Allied Commander had sought to convince his colleagues that the German initiative could be used to the benefit of the Allies. 'This is matter of opportunity for us, not disaster,' he said, before making it clear that, although there were attractions in so doing, he was not going to allow the German forces to extend themselves across the Meuse.

Eisenhower sought to create a major targeted counter-attack, and he needed Patton to undertake it. George Patton had never been one to stand in the shadows when he could be in the spotlight and he readily agreed to the order that he should detour through Luxembourg and drive through the southern flank of the German advance. Such was his desire to be actively involved in delivering this riposte that he undertook to turn his men and be ready to attack on 22 December. This bravado was treated sceptically by others in the room, but, with Eisenhower's warning that his advance should be well thought through and methodical, the grinning Patton set about making the telephone calls that would put the necessary changes under way.

Before the end of the day the Supreme Allied Commander would decide to divide the battle-zone into two, the better to spread the defensive load across the Ardennes front. He would appoint Montgomery to share the work with Bradley, the former coming into the arena to take charge of the northern sector, leaving Bradley to command in the south. It was a controversial decision, but a decisive one; no debate, despite the anger many Americans would feel, the injured pride of his good friend Omar Bradley and increased difficulties for himself in keeping two senior men happy and focused in such a situation. Justifiably on grounds of merit, though surely to ease the pain his colleague must be feeling, Eisenhower sent a request to Washington that Bradley be promoted to four star General.

The operation that Patton was to direct was of little value to those defending St-Vith and those believing their stand at Wiltz could protect the town of Bastogne, nine miles to the west. Indeed, faced with no chance of reinforcements arriving in time and relying on foot messengers to communicate with the new command post at Sibret, just south-west of Bastogne, the officers in Wiltz divided their men into small groups to make their way back to Bastogne and Sibret. It would be a tortuous journey for all and the last for many.

As news of Wiltz being sacrificed reached Bastogne, those who had sought the town as refuge felt the sick emotion of being faced with a repetition of their battles for survival. The units that had been sent out to the east and north of the town to block roads and generally hamper German forward movement had been badly hit, the team at Noville and those at Wardin, just three miles east of Bastogne centre, all but wiped out.

The need to defend the town would surely begin in earnest the following day and there was much panic among the residents and the troops. The locals couldn't believe that the war had come back again, and those soldiers as yet unblooded were listening to the talk of those who had survived four terrible days of assault. The rank and file, like their officers, had neither expected the attack nor been well prepared for it.

In London, Winston Churchill took a call from Eisenhower advising him of the inclusion of Montgomery in the new dual command arrangement; Churchill assured him that British forces would be pleased to contribute to the spiking of

Right: Digging in was a matter of personal survival for many Americans and had to be undertaken in dreadful conditions, often despite the nearby presence of a dead colleague.

Hitler's ambitions. One of Montgomery's first moves had been to reverse his repositioning of his 21 Army Group forces destined for an attack into the Rhineland and move some units south towards the Ardennes because he considered reinforcements coming from the United Kingdom might not arrive in time to prevent 1st SS Panzer from crossing the Meuse. This prudent move was typical of his pre-planning and good order; he was uncomfortable with, as he put it, the situation that 'remained unpleasantly vague'.

Such was the concern that the Meuse, Hitler's prime short-term target, was susceptible that emergency deployments were made between Liège, Dinant and Givet involving reconnaissance units from the British Special Air Service and armoured car patrols, while Brussels itself witnessed teams building barriers and roadblocks. Montgomery's assessment was that the Germans were close to achieving their goal of getting across the Meuse and heading for Brussels.

Having said that, in his personal command post far back from the front, Adolf Hitler was not in a state of unfettered euphoria. He glared at the operational map of 'Wacht am Rhein' and weighed pluses with minuses, good news with bad. Dietrich had struggled but was still giving strident assurances of imminent success, Skorzeny had been unable to implement Hitler's own plan to the degree intended – though rumours of his activity had done almost as much damage as if he had completed it as planned – and the only constant that suited him was that the suffocatingly low cloud and mist had persisted and so kept the Allied aircraft out of the equation. His meteorologists had been right and he surely needed just two or three more days of the same conditions to see his plan succeed. If that was Hitler's wish, perhaps Eisenhower, and certainly hundreds of his front-line officers, preceded their attempts to sleep with a little prayer for clear skies soon.

20 DECEMBER

The arrival of Montgomery at General Courtney Hodges' headquarters in Chaudefontaine was eagerly awaited. The mild-mannered commander of First Army had just faced the biggest military challenge of his career and had not disgraced himself for, though he was initially as convinced as others that the German attacks were minor acts of a desperate army and probably had no ambition beyond distracting the Allied plans for crossing the Rhine, the moment he realised their intensity he had acted. He had mustered all the men he could and concentrated on defence, creating a worthy barrier from the Belgian–German border at Monschau in a wide sweep around the Elsenborn Ridge to Stavelot. Although Peiper had driven south of these positions it had not benefited him and the delays forced on the German units east of Elsenborn could yet prove decisive.

Hodges certainly welcomed the commitment shown by Montgomery's new role and was eager to get back on to the offensive. His current thinking was to confront the main thrust of the German salient with a push towards Vielsalm and he suspected the British commander would concur. Upon his arrival, however,

Montgomery demonstrated his independence by taking reports from his own liaison officers that he had sent out the night before to obtain their own information on the state of play in the action areas of which he was to take control.

Using the data gleaned, Montgomery suggested that the German movement would soon veer north, in the direction of Liège and that, therefore, early attacks were not practicable; he wanted the troops in the St-Vith pocket to be withdrawn and, as he put it, have the battlefield 'tidied up'. In this he returned to his long-held belief that once an enemy's attack had passed the first stages no counter-attack should be considered until a new defensive line had been created and the enemy's strength, potential and likely ambitions had been identified. He showed little enthusiasm for, as he deemed it, wasting men on Hodges' planned attack towards Vielsalm and seemed to be favouring his strategy employed in the Desert and Normandy where the enemy should be allowed to advance beyond its capabilities, be stopped at that point, and then destroyed. As this unexpected philosophy was being debated a message came through from Brigadier General Robert Hasbrouck in St-Vith outlining the position there and making it clear that, with additional help, he felt he could still defend this important town. As a result, it was agreed that efforts should be made to reach him though, Montgomery insisted, Ridgway and his XVIII Corps should still pass through Vielsalm and help ensure a safe exodus from St-Vith thereby shortening the defence line.

During the day the defenders of St-Vith felt the claustrophobic presence of ever-encroaching German forces as the 62nd Volksgrenadiers arrived from the south, the 2nd and 9th SS Panzer divisions were driving enthusiastically closer, having been re-directed from Dietrich's army by an order from Hitler himself, and, from the east, the 18th Volksgrenadiers and the Führer Escort Brigade were getting themselves into a position to strike. Once he received the confirmation from Hodges that Ridgway's men were hurrying towards him in support, Bob Hasbrouck became ever more determined to hold out.

It should be remembered that the weather by this time was particularly harsh, with severe night frosts and hour upon hour of heavy snow falling from leaden skies. The ground, now often frozen hard, was easing tank movement; the lesser roads and tracks that had been churned into mud-baths by Panther and Tiger tracks, now were like concrete and the German vehicles could move at greater pace, and often off-road.

All around Bastogne the Allied defences were crumbling, either by sacrificing positions or having roadblocks and outposts overrun. In most instances withdrawal was only ordered as a last resort and for strong military reasons. As the battle for the Ardennes had developed there were fewer examples of panic or nervous retreat among the raw or tired American units, indeed a thousand feats of group or individual bravery contributed to the sturdy defence the Germans were encountering.

The fall of Bastogne was already being predicted, although for the bluff, no-nonsense Anthony McAuliffe there was still a fight to be won. The town he protected was almost surrounded – his forces controlled only one road, the one to Neufchâteau to the south-west where VIII Corps had set up its new command post. He considered that an attempted breakout would put the lives of his men at greater risk than if he stayed put. He knew that more German forces were being brought into the area, but knew too that American reinforcements were also on their way; it was simply a question of holding on. He felt he could do this for at least another two days, especially if he kept road contact with the command post, but this was a vain hope; by late afternoon, the Germans had managed to cut it and he and his men were utterly surrounded.

The reckless pursuit of personal glory, using his interpretation of his Führer's orders to ignore a more measured advance, had seen Jochen Peiper allow his group to be completely cut off. He had carried too little fuel, ammunition and food to support such a rapid drive and the remainder of 1st SS Panzer was still struggling to get across the Amblève. The young officer was embroiled in staving off assaults from units of 3rd Armored Division and 82nd Airborne; tough fighter though he was, Peiper had brought about his own downfall, which was imminent. His pleas for supplies could not be met; his impetuosity had served the Führer badly.

21 DECEMBER

The sixth day of the Ardennes offensive saw the beginning of a switch of impetus. Although the Germans were sending wave after wave of heavy armour and infantry against American positions, the defence although desperate was now more orderly. The German advance units must be delayed long enough for the substantial American reserves to arrive and balance the equation. If the attackers broke through easily they would remain strong and even get too far ahead of the approaching Allied forces currently *en route* from north and south; if the enemy could be continually delayed to the point of exhaustion, so much the better for the fresh troops.

Montgomery was bringing not only a different level of battlefield experience to the situation, but also a diversity of strategy that was somewhat foreign to American officers. Although Eisenhower, Bradley and Patton all understood the possible value of giving ground in order to strike more efficiently at a later point, the middle-ranking American officer and his men, with little knowledge of strategy and tactics, found this a very odd policy. To date in this dreadful contest there had been little thought of giving ground so as to get the opponent to over-extend himself. Peiper had not needed any help to achieve such a situation, but the Americans were reluctant to give up territory anywhere.

In the north, Dietrich was mounting diverse attacks at Malmédy and elsewhere. Otto Skorzeny, his special forces experts now being used as conventional infantry and tank units, failed in his attempt to break into the town and had to retreat. A little to the east, 1st Division positions at Butgenbach were finally broken after hours of attack by German tanks, but no sooner had the attackers poured through the resulting gap than their tanks were picked off by accurate fire which ended this offensive for the time being.

There were also examples of lost opportunities on the part of German forward units; it seems that the farther they got into the campaign and the closer they came to the barrier of the Meuse, the more cautious and wary they became. For some units, such as General Krüger's LVIII Panzer Corps, the early euphoria of disposing of American defenders gave way to uncertainty with, in Krüger's case, an opportunity to cross the Ourthe being lost through undue caution.

Below: A typical scene just before and after Christmas 1944. A German tank crew ignores a stream of American prisoners.

The Peiper situation was becoming an embarrassment to the German High Command for, though it could be argued that adjacent and following forces had not kept pace with the young hero, his mindless race for glory was now heading for disaster. At Stoumont, Peiper was half-way to the Meuse, but unable to proceed without re-supply and was about to be attacked by three battalions.

But the defenders of St-Vith would have taken some convincing that the battle was going their way. By early evening they were confronting forces ten times their own number, and while some of the senior officers believed that they could hold out until morning, they could not ignore the regular reports that suggested the contrary and became conscious of important defensive positions having to be abandoned in the face of awesome tank and artillery barrages. There were instances where the fire reached beyond those seeking to withdraw, with command posts being overrun and instructions issued one minute becoming redundant the next. There was some panic; whatever extra firepower the Americans brought into the town was being immediately knocked out by enveloping German fire and there were examples of American tank crews trying to ram Tigers and Panthers as they raced through the defensive lines.

Some American units were hurried back to positions west of the town in the hope that stronger defences could be created while the Germans were mopping-up. Others remained in the beleaguered command posts where, at about midnight, it was decided to effect a fighting withdrawal on the defences being set up. They would indeed have to fight their way out because the Germans were now between them and their objective, and the soldiers emerging from their foxholes and hiding-places clambered aboard the armoured troop carriers to avoid annihilation in the town of St-Vith, now back in German hands after a long, tortuous defence.

BASTOGNE:
THE TURNING POINT

For many reasons, including that for some it featured a reputation-enhancing performance by the charismatic George Patton, Bastogne is always highlighted as a dominant feature in the Battle of the Bulge; this book will not break the trend, though the action around the town undoubtedly included bad errors by both sides and, to some extent, seems an unlikely case for glorification.

Just six days after the German forces had begun their Ardennes offensive, Bastogne was surrounded by General von Lüttwitz's XLVII Panzer Corps. It was as much an island as St-Vith had become, but it was a more vital prize for the German forces bent on controlling the region as they pressed on towards the Meuse and Antwerp. Walther Model could not simply ignore the situation there, much though he would have preferred to continue his advance to the north and south without this distraction. The Allies, now conscious of the German intention to break through this lightly manned portion of their front, had other priorities too, but could not leave General McAuliffe and his modest numbers of airborne and armoured units to be overrun or left to hold out until such time as it would serve the wider Allied purpose to rescue them.

Bastogne presented a 'Catch 22' situation to both sides. For the Germans the town was the vital hub of the road network. and if captured quickly would speed their advance and enhance their supply routes. But the more troops they committed to its capture the fewer could contribute to the front-line push. The Americans understood this and wanted to use Bastogne first to delay the enemy and later as a springboard for resuming the offensive. The encircling German units needed to secure the town before the Americans brought in reinforcements.

It has been debated for more than fifty years whether the Germans could and should have by-passed Bastogne in strength, leaving sufficient forces there to prevent McAuliffe from breaking out. Similarly, it has been argued that the Allies could have been more imaginative in countering the German action in this sector and might have supported the troops in the town in other ways; after all, Allied strategy was not opposed to allowing the German forces to overstretch themselves along narrow lines of speedy advance which they could neither defend nor supply.

In the event, Bastogne was virtually encircled. Von Lüttwitz, had elements of four divisions at his disposal. Detachments of 2nd Panzer had been held back from their main advance to threaten from the north, 5th Parachute Division were blocking the southern perimeter and General Kokott's 26th Volksgrenadier Division and a Panzergrenadier regiment of Panzer Lehr were close by to launch the attack. McAuliffe was maintaining a spirited and skilful defence, but it seemed probable that only a dramatic improvement in airborne supplies or an earlier than expected arrival of Patton from the south, or both, could save him and his men from surrender. The Americans' situation was dire, but as yet certainly did not call for capitulation, but apparently von Lüttwitz thought otherwise and he initiated one of the most celebrated battlefield exchanges of the war.

Unconvinced that the German forces could take the town without serious losses, von Lüttwitz had General Kokott send someone to call on the Americans to surrender. On 22 December the lowly Lieutenant Helmuth Henke went forward with three other officers under a flag of truce. His first contact was with Sergeant Oswald Butler of 327th Glider Infantry Regiment who was on sentry duty in an isolated farmhouse on the road into the town from the south. Having established that the quartet had a message for his commanding general, the resourceful Butler tore up the white flag to make blindfolds and led two of the Germans to Colonel Joe Harper who quickly advised McAuliffe's acting Chief of Staff. A few minutes later the message was being translated for McAuliffe:

To the USA Commander of the encircled town of Bastogne.

The fortune of war is changing. This time the USA forces in and near Bastogne have been encircled by strong German armoured units.

There is only one possibility to save the encircled USA troops from total annihilation: that is the honourable surrender of the encircled town.

If this proposal should be rejected, one German Artillery Corps and six AA Battalions are ready to annihilate the USA troops in and near Bastogne.

All the serious civilian losses caused by this artillery fire would not correspond with the well-known American humanity.

McAuliffe is reported to have laughed and said, 'Aw, nuts!', and immediately left to visit some men in the front line who had accounted for a German roadblock. On his return he was reminded that the two emissaries were still waiting and that this formal communication merited an official reply. When he asked his officers present what he should say, they felt that his first remark couldn't be bettered. Colonel Harper handed over the document, which read:

To the German Commander
Nuts!
The American Commander

To the pompous and patronising German officers he explained that it meant they could 'go to Hell'. He added that if the attack continued his men would kill 'every goddamned German' who tried to get in. The Germans saluted and left with the comment, 'We will kill many Americans.'

One wonders why von Lüttwitz made this move. It has been suggested that he had come to believe the Führer's propaganda that the American troops were fine when advancing without opposition, but would be vulnerable if they encountered setbacks. But surely he must have known that this was nonsense, given the relentless drive across France from Normandy until now. He may, of course, have been feeling the pressure of the static situation around the town; siege tactics did not sit easily alongside the Führer's plan.

Perhaps he should be given more credit. He must have known that there were scant resources backing his advance and may have doubted the wisdom of waiting for reinforcements that might or might not arrive. Perhaps he felt that he had nothing to lose by suggesting that the enemy surrender.

It is not surprising that the Americans rejected the idea. They were confident that they could hold the town and certain of relief at some early point. They were not overly concerned about the inhabitants who, warmly housed and with adequate food supplies, were mainly worried about the threat of re-occupation; they would certainly not have wanted the Americans to surrender.

It should be borne in mind that, with the German offensive only one week old, there remained some confusion in the Allied High Command. Eisenhower was still at Versailles and the implementation of his orders had yet to bear fruit; his mood matched the weather which remained overcast and gloomy; forecasts were that it would not improve sufficiently for Allied aircraft to exert their advantage for some days yet.

THE GERMAN DEFENCE OF BASTOGNE

At McAuliffe's command post in the north-west sector of Bastogne there was quiet satisfaction that they were holding the situation, but the need to get more supplies through was growing in importance. A message was received saying that Major General Hugh Gaffey's 4th Armored Division was approaching the town on the left flank of Patton's III Corps' drive, and another suggested that air supplies would begin later that day.

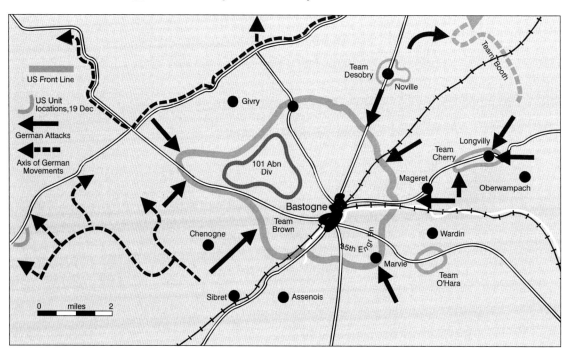

The delay in capturing the town was now playing on German nerves. Not only was von Manteuffel livid at von Lüttwitz for his attempt to secure a surrender, principally because it contained threats that he couldn't fulfil, but he was also angry that General Bayerlein was showing no initiative to the south-west. He ordered the latter to leave one regiment at Bastogne to support the envelopment exercise and push the remainder forward in the attacks to the south. Now, however, he was going to have to find a way of making good von Lüttwitz's unauthorised threat; it would help if he could get support from the air for he was not blessed with the firepower that would displace the Americans as long as they had ammunition.

In fact, the defenders had very little ammunition of any sort. McAuliffe, whose wit we have already seen, is reported to have told one commander asking for more artillery, 'If you see 400 Germans in a hundred-yard area, and they have their heads up, you can fire artillery at them, but no more than two rounds.' The news that intended air drops had had to be postponed because of continuing bad weather made matters worse. McAuliffe and his colleagues could only hope that the piecemeal attacks by the Germans to date were indicative that they too were short of supplies.

That night German bombers flew over Bastogne, and the desperate defenders of the town had another reason to feel abandoned; if the Luftwaffe was in the air where were their own aircraft? Their low spirits were raised within hours, however, when dawn on 23 December brought a bright sun and a blue sky to the freezing scene. Soon Allied fighters swept across the town on their way to other missions and, shortly afterwards, the throaty roar of transport aircraft was heard. Paratroops jumped from them, and soon the ground had been prepared for the dropping of supplies. By mid-morning, fighters were being directed to German targets and knocking out tanks and armoured cars without opposition and by noon a fleet of bull-nosed C-47 transports was overhead. Several of these mercy flights were downed by German anti-aircraft units, but the mission continued, the sky awash with parachutes supporting their precious cargoes. It was a sight for sore eyes, and chilled bones; desperate men … and the residents of the beleaguered town joined in the celebration.

That same morning, the Germans, stirred into action by von Manteuffel, had made some brief advances in the south-west corner of the town before their tanks and infantry were forced back. The Allied forces were buoyed by the supply drop but they knew that they still needed Patton and his men to arrive, and quickly.

George Patton preferred to move fast and he liked to meet expectations – his own and other people's. Despite his individualism he was a team player, and when the call had come to relieve Bastogne he had focused on only two benefits – to show his expertise in swift battlefield manoeuvring and give support to the cause. Initially, every decision he made, every order he gave, was effective; he showed remarkable dexterity and determination in redeploying the element of his army designated to move on Bastogne. Very rapidly the troops destined for the isolated town were in place and on the move. But he had not kept his plans secure from enemy intercepts, was using untested troops and, of course, had not had time to plan as accurately as he would have done given different circumstances.

Initially progress of III Corps to Bastogne was painfully slow, by Patton's own terms at least, and the Germans were able to make many attempts to block him. It took four days to achieve what he had planned to take two, and, by the time he reached the town, US 4th Armored Division had already arrived, bringing tanks, infantry weapons and supplies.

The battle for Bastogne had, it can be argued, been won the moment the skies cleared and the Allied transports could fly in supplies, though for 48 hours both sides benefited from ground and air reinforcements. Then, Brandenberger's Seventh Army was dislodged by Patton's XII Corps and the week-long siege was over. The relief of the town gave a wonderful fillip to Allied morale, especially to the Americans who had come so close to what for them would have been a major loss. But it was a wretched failure for the Germans. Not only had their ground units failed to force home the initiative when they had it, but the event had again showed that the Luftwaffe was no longer a factor in the overall battle. When Allied flights reached Bastogne on 24 December, the Commander of 5th Parachute Division, General Hulmann, complained that 'Not a single German aircraft appeared'; Adolf Galland would later identify the Ardennes as the time when the Luftwaffe was finally finished as a fighting force.

Like St-Vith and other specific battle points in 'Wacht am Rhein', Bastogne would not be the cause of victory or defeat in the Battle of the Bulge, but it was to prove a turning-point. It would have been a massive prize, however temporary, for the Germans and its loss could have affected American morale for a time. Its retention, with all that entailed, energised American spirits and the status quo that had stood at the moment Hitler gave the go-ahead for his Ardennes Offensive would be quickly regained. The Americans lost many dead and suffered thousands of casualties, but the Germans lost one in five of their men who took part. The Allies could replace their sad losses, but the Germans dead were irreplaceable. For the Germans, Bastogne was a wretched loss in every way.

22 DECEMBER

Considering that St-Vith had fallen, Bastogne was under extreme pressure, and Peiper's men were a full twenty miles farther west, the fact that Sepp Dietrich, Hitler's trusted factotum of so many years' standing, was still trying to get clear of the Elsenborn Ridge as dawn broke on this sixth day of the German offensive was desperate news for Hitler. By now he should have been spearheading the advance around the inside of the giant curve that would take the German Army to its goal.

Now, finally, a combination of German tanks pierced the ranks of 1st Division near Butgenbach and it seemed the job was done as men and machines dashed towards and through the half-mile gap. Again, however, Dietrich was to be thwarted as other units from the same Division poured bazooka fire into the rampaging tanks and destroyed infantry groups with accurate fire. A curved line of defence barely five miles wide, made up of the 1st, 2nd and 99th Infantry Divisions had stopped the Germans' principal thrust just a few miles from its own border. It was a massive achievement and one that signalled the end of Dietrich's war as he withdrew ignominiously with the loss of more than one hundred tanks and thousands of men standing as a testament to his inadequacies as a major battlefield commander. For all his rhetoric and personal drive, his shortcomings in respect of strategic theory and tactical use of men and machines had found him out. Already humbled by his under-performance and the insult of Hitler's handing over to von Manteuffel the two divisions that had been due to follow his intended breakthrough, the one-time butcher might have expected this to be his last senior battlefield role, but he was to be given an Eastern Front command within weeks, though he achieved no greater success there. His physical toughness and his cries to arms counted for little; in the Ardennes his Sixth Panzer lost 23,451 men.[8] He had been given the best quality of men in the three Armies deployed by Hitler and had good reserves, but his own desire for fame and achievement brought a reluctance to share in the potential 'prize' and opportunities were lost to the detriment of the national cause.

The two divisions that had been intended to follow Dietrich's advance had helped hasten the demise of St-Vith and now 9th Panzer was heading for Vielsalm and 2nd Panzer was dangerously close to cutting the lines of the XVIII Airborne Corps, having by-passed Vielsalm before veering north. Had they been brought out in support of von Manteuffel earlier instead of, as von Rundstedt assessed it, keeping them behind Sixth Panzer 'for the purpose of giving Colonel-General Dietrich the chance of a magnificent victory', the outcome might have been different. The veteran Prussian considered 'it unbalanced the entire offensive and jeopardised a potential victory'.

At this point the commanders of the American forces were becoming increasingly concerned that many of their men had had five days of continuous fighting in dreadful conditions against, more often than not, superior firepower and numbers. A good portion of these had not fought in Europe before and none had suffered an Ardennes winter. There were numerous instances of wounded men having to be called from medical areas to join the fight, of petrol running out and ammunition being rationed.

The town of Vielsalm was occupying Matthew Ridgway's thoughts; if German pressure on the road to the west of the town became a breakthrough his line would be dissected with dreadful ramifications for the troops occupying ground to the east where a substantial American salient was being created. He drove with Robert Hasbrouck to a meeting with General Bruce Clarke to the east of

Commanster, and then called General Bill Hoge to assure him that he would find a way to get him and his men out of the salient that night. Ridgway had become unimpressed with the negative attitudes he was finding among his senior men, but felt that Hasbrouck was the most likely to summon the strength of will and level of support to get what equated to two full divisions out through a narrow neck of Allied territory.

Still contributing to Allied discomfort was another aspect of the Ardennes winter – low cloud and persistent mists that shrouded high and low ground, and the meteorologists offered no positive news of it lifting. It had dulled moods, restricted battlefield visibility and, as Hitler had intended, kept Allied aircraft grounded. Given this advantage the German plans could and should have worked better, but continued logistical failings, the results of using such a mongrel mix of nationalities and troops of contrasting experience, and the failings of certain commanders had evened matters out. By comparison, the inexperienced in the American ranks had chiefly acted with discipline and followed orders, even surrendering with great reluctance when being told that they could not fight on.

Von Manteuffel, having driven some fifteen miles west of Bastogne the day before, could not understand why Bayerlein could not do the same, and he was incandescent with rage at the thought of von Lüttwitz's 'surrender demand'.

As the day of 22 December darkened into another dank and bitterly cold night, Hasbrouck was sending details of the evacuation of the American salient to the troops at the front, and until dawn and after, some 20,000 men with tanks and other vehicles wove an unhappy path west and north-west back through the lines around Vielsalm. Few of them relished the move, but it was an extraordinary example of clear orders being effectively implemented, and it meant exhausted forces being saved to fight another day rather than being sacrificed for little gain. It was precisely the clear thinking, even if it had come with an element of desperation, that was beginning to desert the Germans. It was the 'tidying up' of the battlefield that Montgomery sought.

23 DECEMBER

The American withdrawal to and past Vielsalm continued into the morning. The routes they needed to take were not ideal, but for once the bitter weather was to their advantage for the rock-hard ground speeded up the pace; only two tanks were sacrificed where, in milder conditions, they would have become bogged-down. At various points there were still fierce engagements with the enemy but the withdrawal was achieved despite the misgivings of those involved.

For the first time in a long while the night sky had been clear in the Ardennes, with a resulting fall in temperature, from severe cold to deep freeze. The sky remained clear and by daybreak the sun was making its long-awaited appearance. Soon its heat would thaw the ground over which Hasbrouck was mounting his withdrawal, but even he realised this would be a momentous day; if it remained clear the Allied aircraft would fly!

Indeed, at dawn light the fighter-pilots and bomber crews were already in the air, destined to bring joy to their colleagues and the local populace and dread to the German forces below them. As the Allies celebrated the change of weather, Hitler and Model must have feared what it would bring; what it brought was more than 1,300 flights from Ninth Army Air Force alone!

With Bastogne receiving supply drops by midday and the retreat past Vielsalm going well, the Allies were justified in their relief and newly found confidence, but they were still well aware of the advancing German forces. The 2nd Panzer Division that had by-passed Vielsalm and come close to cutting the road to the west was now being re-focused to make for the main road between Bastogne and Liège, for if they could reach and use that the race to the Meuse could be quickened. They headed for the isolated hamlet of Baraque de Fraiture which sat astride the highway and had been under occasional attack in recent days from LVIII Panzer Corps as it moved past what it assumed to be a minor defence point. In fact, the few stone houses had become a gathering-point for various armoured vehicles and personnel withdrawing from action farther east, and by now howitzers, self-propelled guns, multiple .50cal machine-guns, an anti-aircraft battalion and a reconnaissance company were stationed there.

Even this motley crew would be insufficient to stave off 2nd Panzer if they chose to attack in strength, and prompt action by Major General Gavin, commander of 82nd Airborne Division saw extra men being rushed to the area, though by early afternoon still more reinforcements were needed. If the Germans were successful here their onward path to Liège could cut off a huge number of American forces.

This German initiative was not only demonstrating much determination but also threatening the newly arrived Montgomery's declared strategy of forming a perimeter around the battle-zone in his area, whose troops should serve as a deterrent until the area farther east had been modified to his liking. German units were reported west of Marche, some 25 miles nearer the Meuse than those at Baraque de Fraiture, and now the generals charged with implementing Monty's policy were confused, some forming their own tactics 'on the hoof' as they sought to stave of the German thrusts.

The remarkable but ill-considered dash for the Meuse by Jochen Peiper was drawing to a close near Stoumont. He may have followed his Führer's instructions more precisely than had Dietrich, but so small, and now isolated, an advance had been foolish. In his current position at La Gleize, Peiper was being bombarded by howitzers and a 155mm gun under the command of General Harrison who reported to Ridgway that he would mount a final attack from a better position the following day. The German hero was not prepared to wait for that and radioed for permission to pull out, if necessary without his vehicles and the wounded. Failing to get agreement, the impulsive young fellow again showed his independence and ordered the withdrawal anyway.

The evacuation of American troops from the salient east of Vielsalm had ploughed on throughout the day with those manning the exit points eagerly watching for the last of the American units before making off themselves to allow the rearguard cover of Task Force Jones through from the south. The Germans, long since wise to the withdrawal plan, were now bombarding the exit points just south of Salmchâteau, and Colonel Nelson, sure that all the troops that were supposed to have passed his position there had done so, was constantly radioing for permission to withdraw. Failing to get an answer of any kind the Colonel ordered his 112th Regiment to move, but no sooner had his men sought to get onto the main road to Vielsalm than they discovered the vehicles of the Task Force were already there and the resulting traffic jam slowed the convoy considerably. The failure in communication – Hasbrouck had thought his agreement for Nelson to withdraw had reached the colonel some hours before – now meant that the slow-moving columns were prime targets for German shells as they snaked up the hill to Salmchâteau.

By dark the vehicles of the Task Force and the 112th were busy trying to find alternative routes west that would save them from the German shelling, the former finding themselves embroiled in close-quarter fighting in the village of Provedroux after they had found a route across the Salm. Nelson found a different way but also got across the river.

At Vielsalm, Hasbrouck had already evacuated his schoolhouse command post as German tanks began to fire into the main streets, and now the last units were leaving the town and laying charges beneath the bridge over the Salm which they had just crossed to exit the town. With the destruction of the bridge the astonishing operation to withdraw the thousands of men and their vehicles from the salient south of St-Vith had been completed.

At the same time, a communiqué was being sent from Eisenhower to General Hodges asking that Hasbrouck should receive his 'personal message' that 'the magnificent job you are doing is having a great beneficial effect on our whole situation. I am personally grateful to you and wish you would let all of your people know that if they continue to carry out their mission with the splendid spirit they have so far shown, they will have deserved well of their country'. [9]

It was indicative of the missed opportunities of which the Germans were guilty that a jeep carrying several Germans disguised as Americans appeared in Dinant late on this day. In one of very few examples of the clandestine operations and sabotage raids in which Hitler and Skorzeny had placed such faith, the group arrived long after the chance of a German *coup de main* at the Meuse had been lost; they were promptly captured by an astute British roadblock and ended their war with the sole satisfaction that they had at least made it to the river, if not across it.

24 DECEMBER

Early on Christmas Eve morning the advantages to be gained by the Allies in having clearer skies in which to demonstrate their air power superiority had not been fully realised, but they would gradually begin to have an impact. Following the extensive flying activity on the previous day, this one would see even more … at least 2,000 sorties by Ninth Army Air Force. The 2nd Panzer Division was by now closing on Manhay and threatening to move on through the small groups of modest Belgian homes *en route* to Liège. The problem of this being the boundary point between Ridgway and his XVIII Airborne and Collins' VII Corps was exacerbated early on by the P-47 Thunderbolts brought in to stall the German tank columns targeting some of their own ground units trying to do the same. Eventually, the identification procedure worked and several heavy German tanks were knocked out, encouraging Walter Richardson, commanding the units of 3rd Armored Division in the town, to order a company of infantry to the scene of the air attack with the aim of driving the ambitious opposition back to Baraque de Fraiture.

This he did in ignorance of the fact that the loss of nine tanks had barely dented the German forces here and that the enemy had simply reversed, veered to the west and by-passed the roadblock. The reinforcements were being sent to a point where there was no enemy.

Meanwhile, farther north in his newly established headquarters, Matthew Ridgway was finding a way of strengthening the remaining mini-bulge in 82nd Airborne's line between Trois Ponts and Manhay – it still extended almost to Vielsalm. As he planned the movement of supplementary offensive forces, Bernard Montgomery arrived demanding that his creed of making the battlefield map appear more orderly was implemented. He insisted that the 82nd be withdrawn and the bulge reduced to a straight, more easily defended line.

If he found Ridgway reluctant to comply, Montgomery got a still more hostile reception when he drove on to Courtney Hodges' command post at Tongres. His announcement that Collins' VII Corps could deploy to defend a line between Hotton and Andenne on the Meuse was not well received by a General who, like most of his colleagues, was not fond of the military theory of *reculer pour mieux sauter*. The British field marshal stressed his desire to avoid immediate contact with the enemy, but to let him come forward, perhaps outstripping his supply line, and then counter-attack in circumstances most favourable to the Allied forces.

The Americans had not enjoyed a good working relationship with Montgomery, and Eisenhower was almost alone among them in being able to ignore any dislike of his strange personality and take advantage of his generalship. Here his record was undeniably good, though more than one historian has come to class him as only modestly successful and Martin Blumenson describes him as 'the most over-rated general of World War Two'.[10] Despite his haughty demeanour and rather dismissive air, Montgomery persuaded his men to be confident and patient. For one of his disposition and character he was surprisingly adept at enthusing the rank and file.

Monty didn't wait around for debate but left some despondent senior officers as he moved on. However stretched VII Corps was at the moment, it was the feeling among the Americans that the German advance was running out of steam, in fact running out of petrol, ammunition and provisions, and this was endorsed when news reached Collins' deputy, General Palmer, that 2nd Armored Division believed that they had much of 2nd Panzer in a pocket and vulnerable to a hard attack. Some confusion followed as messages between Hodges' HQ staff and officers at the front, but eventually the directive became fully understood, that Collins was to not undertake offensive missions but should seek to stabilise the right flank of First Army and be prepared to withdraw to a line between Andenne, Hotton and Manhay as and when he considered it necessary.

But 'Lightning Joe' Collins was not in the mood to accept that good battlefield opportunities should be ignored. He sought the views of his staff before telling Hodges' courier that, taking sole responsibility for his actions, he was determined to proceed with an attack on the 2nd Panzer units he considered ripe for the taking, and he transmitted the decision to General Harmon, who had been pressing for the agreement to attack.

The dire circumstances at Bastogne and the wretchedly slow progress of Dietrich earlier was encouraging thought among the German battlefield generals that a change of plan was called for. Peiper's dash had come to a halt and had done little to improve the humour of such as von Manteuffel and other seasoned commanders. Jodl was back with Hitler at the Führer's headquarters and becoming increasingly unnerved by reports from the front; he knew that Hitler's moods were fluctuating between determined enthusiasm at every item of modest good news and deep despair when anyone deigned to speak of reversals. Now he was fielding strident requests from von Manteuffel for a complete change of policy. The latter knew of the logistical weaknesses that had dogged the campaign, of the losses his forces had suffered during their hard advance and that the spearhead of 2nd Panzer Division was now fully fourteen miles ahead of its rearguard; his own current location, in a château near La Roche, was under attack as he spoke. The 2nd Panzer was so vulnerable to counter-attack from the side, and now to a strafing from the skies, that he was urg-

Right: 101st Airborne Division moves out of Bastogne during the siege.

ing Jodl to allow him to confront the Allied units to the *east* of the Meuse rather than continue with the plan to cross the river and head for Antwerp. He must have agreement to this change of plan now if he was to prevent the enemy from reforming and redeploying. All he could persuade Jodl to do was get Hitler's view of the suggestion; both men knew it would not be well received.

Just ten miles north of von Manteuffel's position, the tangled messages and battle-zone flux was causing chaos among the ranks of American forces supposedly 'tidying up' Montgomery's battlefield by forming a new defensive line. Several Task Force groups south of Manhay were overwhelmed by tank attacks and the resulting withdrawal was rather more confused than Montgomery would have liked. The weather was poor; it was to be a very white Christmas as snow flurries gave way to heavy falls, occasionally swirled by gusts of wind. It was a night when thoughts of a celebratory Christmas Day were far from the minds of desperate American infantry and tank crews; a good number of them would not survive this dire Christmas Eve night.

25 DECEMBER

The Battle of the Bulge was about to reach its zenith as the first rays of dawn heralded Christmas Day of 1944. At its farthest point the 'Bulge' had reached the south-eastern approaches of Celles, just five miles from the town of Dinant on the Meuse, that river which these advanced echelons of German troops should

have crossed some days before. General Harmon and his 2nd Armored Division were planning an attack on the stationary German force and sent teams to attack their front and rear.

But this did not signal an all-out counter by the Allies for Montgomery, who had ordered the demolition charges to be removed from the Meuse bridges as early as the 23rd, was still urging defence until the enemy was exhausted. Indeed, in this strange 'fallow' period of the action in the Ardennes there were examples where both armies were pulling back, and a morning conference between Bradley and the field marshal confirmed that this was acceptable to Montgomery, and Bradley flew back to Luxembourg disappointed that such a strategy was still being pursued.

This Christmas morning meant different things to different people around the Ardennes battlefield. Some Allied troops, having been set in defensive mode by Montgomery's orders and currently in a safe position, were able to relax a little, with extra rations being found wherever possible, but others were in the midst of attacking manoeuvres and more were suffering the results of capture. Jochen Peiper was suffering the indignity of withdrawal which, though undertaken without permission and surely a sensible move on his part, was not what he wanted to be doing on this special day. Hasso von Manteuffel was enjoying a sparse meal at La Roche where he had met Major Johann-Meyer, an emissary from the Führer, in an attempt to hasten clearance for his desired change of policy.

Communication with Jodl brought no decision other than that, after continued pressing from von Manteuffel, just one more armoured division would be provided on the understanding that this would enable him to continue his advance.

The German Intelligence reports in the build-up to Christmas had been suggesting that the Allies would not be in a position to mount a significant counterattack against the front of the German thrust until 1 January and until then only bothersome strikes against the flanks could be expected. This counted for little in some quarters, especially for von Manteuffel, who had yet to take Bastogne and was still far behind schedule. Reports from the forefront of the drive to the Meuse at Celles suggested that no further advances could be made until more men could be got to that sector.

BOXING DAY TO NEW YEAR

As a good deal of chaos continued to affect the Ardennes, the second day of Christmas at least brought more Allied air activity, with many German strongpoints coming under fire from potent fighter attacks; a factor that von Rundstedt would later claim to have finally ended the Ardennes adventure. The night had been cold and clear so Allied flights had hardly ceased. This was always likely to bring a change of fortune for the Allied cause and the realisation that moves were afoot to break the Bastogne siege only added to the feeling spreading among their battlefield commanders that the Germans had got as far as they would with their dramatic drive west.

The Americans, particularly Bradley and Patton, were champing at the bit to go on to the offensive rather than continue with the ultra-cautious approach of Montgomery. Of course Patton had undertaken to be in Bastogne by Christmas and was surely smarting at not having achieved this. He did his bit to progress matters now though by agreeing to allow Colonel Creighton Abrams, leading 4th Armored's drive on the town with his 37th Tank Battalion, to attempt the break-through now that air drops were seen to be reaching their compatriots there. Abrams had barely twenty medium tanks but was pressing to make one whole-hearted assault.

Abrams ordered his tanks and halftracks forward, reached the village of Assenois, and, hurried on under the shelter of a creeping artillery barrage. Initial contact with the enemy was sparse and promptly dealt with at close quarters, and by late afternoon the armour had shot its way through all the German resistance it encountered and linked up with men from 326th Engineers, 101st Airborne on the town's outskirts; Bastogne was no longer encircled.

St-Vith, so recently lost to the Germans, was now the target of a heavy onslaught by three hundred aircraft; it was not a battle, it was an annihilation.

Further west, at the extremity of the German advance around Celles, it was rocket-firing Typhoon fighter-bombers that brought an abrupt halt to a German tank group sent forward to assist the push being defended by Harmon's 2nd Division, though more tanks were still being brought up in the vain hope that Hitler's cry of 'to, and over the Meuse' could be realised.

Back from Celles, around the town of Humain where Allied forces were trying to put a stranglehold on the route to their forward units and the enemy was seek-ing to broaden it, the Germans had gained first advantage by forcing the American tank units out of the town past 2nd Panzer equipment they had destroyed in previous days. Then various fruitless attempts to retake the area were made by 4th Cavalry Group before, on 26 December, 9th Panzer Division, with almost 100 tanks and 35 self-propelled guns, arrived from Holland to sup-plement German numbers and aid the push to the Meuse.

The attempts of the replenished forces to get out of Humain and make for Havrenne, and Celles beyond, was disrupted by heavy fire from American tanks, tank-destroyers and artillery, and now Colonel Hinds' Combat Command Reserve entered the fray from the north near Hogne and linked up with Combat Command A. On the morning of the 27th Hinds encircled Humain and, though he found most of the German tanks had been driven out by Allied fire during the night, had to fight long and hard to gain control of the town after which he was helped by P-38 fighter-bombers and flame-throwing Crocodile tanks to clear surrounding pockets of 2nd Panzer Division resistance.

While Hitler was being confronted by a desperate and despondent Alfred Jodl, his much vaunted prediction of a split in the Allied ranks was as close to appearing as it ever would be. Bradley, who until now had taken Montgomery's direction with commendable equanimity, pleaded with Eisenhower's chief of staff, Walter Bedell-Smith, to get Monty to take his foot off the brake, realise the enemy's predicament and press home his advantage. Bedell-Smith, ever the diplomat and knowing his boss was already on his way to Holland to see the British field marshal, declined to agree with his colleague's assessment and assured him that, to the contrary, the Germans could still be over the Meuse in a few hours and the current policy must be persevered with.

It has been the view of many historians, Ronald Lewin[11] included, that no American could match Montgomery in technique and in all that a prepared mind can bring to the battlefield. Although both Bradley and Patton had expressed their readiness to allow the Germans to come on to the Allied lines, exhaust themselves and then be destroyed, it was not really what they wanted to do; it was not in their nature. It seemed illogical to most Americans, who remembered Alamein for very different reasons than the adoring British public, that one should delay in teaching one's opponent a lesson.

The Führer would have been delighted if he had been a party to the Bradley/Bedell-Smith conversation for he was receiving a sad catalogue of negative reports from the front lines ... the Elsenborn Ridge, barely six miles from the Germans' starting-point was still held by American forces; Allied aircraft were in the air in strength and hammering positions throughout the battle-zone; Jochen Peiper – the only man to keep to the intended timing however ill-advised his motives and methods – was close to being cut off and only escaping by ignoring instructions; the farthest point of the German advance, almost within sight of the Meuse, seemed unlikely to break through at Celles without reinforcements; 116th Panzer Division had stopped making progress; the major prize of St-Vith was being destroyed by Allied aircraft, and the catastrophic mismanagement of the Bastogne siege was barely relevant now that the Americans had broken the German ring. At best the advance was temporarily stalled, at worst it was nearing its end.

In brief, the Offensive had lost its momentum. By its own hand it had sacrificed whatever manoeuvrability it had once enjoyed and was foundering at every turn, but out of bravado or foolishness, Hitler was not yet ready to concede. Although surely aware that he had no means of countering the ability of the Allies to fly against, attack and probably destroy any fresh initiatives, he demanded them all the same. His new orders were that Bastogne must be taken, more resolve must be shown in striking forward to and past Manhay and Hotton in support of the forces almost at the Meuse, Brandenberger should push Seventh Army harder in the south and von Manteuffel should arc to the north-east with a view to cutting off the Allied forces caught by this move. It was unfounded opti-

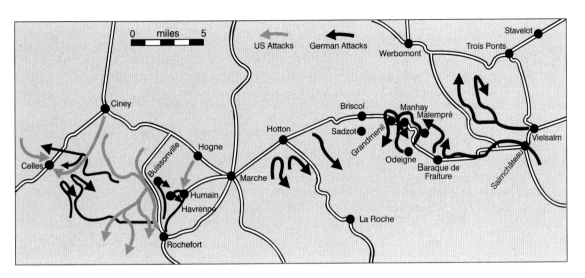

mism, probably based on the fact that the reports he had just received had inevitably and typically been less doom-laden than they might have been. He clung to the chance that a determined riposte to current setbacks would still drive a wedge between British and American commanders and, if the dramatic success he had sought might not be realised, the tactic of attrition could still see him triumph.

THE GERMAN ADVANCE IS STOPPED

Eisenhower decided to meet Montgomery but was delayed because of his train being bombed and by heavy snowfalls, and he would not see him until 28 December. It gave him extra time to prepare for what was likely to be a difficult session. He had to impress on the field marshal the need to keep the entire Allied effort united and positive while realising that the Englishman had inherited forces that were desperately tired and shocked by the events of the last ten days and, at the very least, needed time to regroup and re-equip; he had some sympathy with Montgomery's view that First Army was not yet ready for offensive action. If needed he would have to be firm with the belligerent Patton and his impatient officers; he knew their wish was to press home every advantage ... he shared the same desire.

When the meeting began, Montgomery assured Eisenhower that he had begun planning the advances he would make once he was sure his defences were secure and his men rested and freshly equipped. He said that he had got wind of new German plans to redouble their attacks and assured the Supreme Commander that he did not believe these would be piecemeal or half-hearted. Eisenhower extracted an assurance that Monty would be ready to mount his counter-attacks by New Year's Day or shortly after, and left the meeting feeling that he had obtained the best compromise. He radioed a directive that Omar Bradley should be given 11th Armored and 87th Infantry Divisions and plan an attack in the direction of Houffalize and Bastogne.

**RELIEVING FORCES
APPROACH
BASTOGNE**

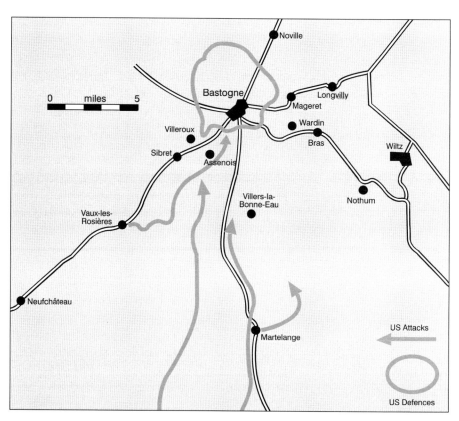

**BASTOGNE
RELIEVED**

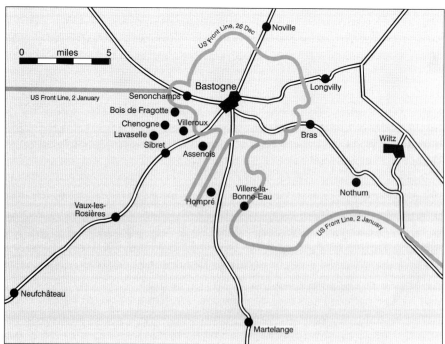

Montgomery moved on to talks with Hodges and afterwards confirmed to Eisenhower that he was not yet able to take the offensive. He cited the fact that there were still pressures on the west flank of his Army and he still needed more men and armour for an advance to be successful. He may have gleaned from the meeting that the Supreme Allied Commander had plenty of concerns occupying him in the south where Patton had not fulfilled his boast about his arrival date at Bastogne; perhaps Monty appreciated that Eisenhower would be wanting to press for success there before forcing him to take the offensive.

One demonstration of the improving situation for the Americans was the performance of General Harmon who had well and truly halted the German spearhead at Celles. In less than 72 hours his 2nd Armored Division had out-thought and out-fought 2nd Panzer to the degree that his list of 'prizes' included 88 tanks and assault guns and 75 heavy guns among more than 400 vehicles captured or destroyed. More than 2,500 of the enemy had been killed or wounded and 1,200 taken prisoner. He could be certain he had stopped the Germans crossing the Meuse, at least at this point.

But elsewhere the local situations were seldom as clear cut. The fracture of the German circle around Bastogne did not necessarily signal the end of the siege and neither did the air drops of fresh supplies; the town would still have to be fought for and Hitler's demand that it must be taken would be filtering through to the troops engaged. In dozens of locations the battle equation was a smaller one with pockets of opposing forces still battling for yards of space, the possession of a farmhouse, or a clear route to their next objective. Much though Montgomery sought to tidy up his battlefield, and even if the Allied aircraft had had a couple of days of clearer weather to exert increasing influence, the Battle of the Bulge remained one of diverse military action with tank movement on a large scale and the deployment of awesome firepower seen alongside small unit warfare and individual acts of heroism.

Indeed, the brighter dawns of recent days had disappeared as suddenly as they had arrived and well before the New Year the days again began with a murky, impenetrable sky across most of the region and fresh persistent heavy snow had smoothed contours and made many roads impassable.

Just as it was exercising Eisenhower's mind, Hitler was again focusing on Bastogne; both men were aware of how crucial this town was to their Ardennes strategy, though by now Hitler must have surely realised that capturing it was not part of a greater prize but the principal gain he could hope for at present. Publicly, he had berated those attending his daily conference for failing to achieve the intended aim of the offensive while adding, perhaps to save his own face bearing in mind his hand was behind its planning, that the great efforts of the German soldiers had secured advantages on the western front that just ten days before could not have been imagined. He vehemently opposed von Rundstedt's proposal of a retreat to a new defensive line east of Bastogne and ordered Model to consolidate his forces ready for a new move on the Meuse. Finally he brightly announced a new plan – Operation 'Nordwind' – which would include new offensives in Alsace against the Allied forces weakened by their counters to 'Wacht am Rhein'.

At Bastogne the 'siege' scenario had long since given way to active combat. Although the town was no longer completely encircled, the initiative demanded by Hitler was due to commence on 30 December: 1st Panzer and 167th Volksgrenadier Divisions would advance from the east and 30th Panzer Lehr and 27th Volksgrenadier Divisions from the north-west. Ammunition and provisions for the defenders had been brought in by road through the mile-wide gap in the German lines, but now glider-borne medical supplies would have to be continued if the new German onslaught was to be beaten off. The time for George Patton's newly provided but rather inexperienced personnel of 11th Armored and 87th Divisions to begin the relieving action was drawing near.

Shortly after midnight on 30 December, forward units of the new American force were within a mile of Bastogne. But now their eagerness overcame them, and logistical misunderstandings caused delays that were to imperil these new and untried troops for the German pincer movement was pressuring their positions from both east and west. If von Manteuffel could close the gap which the

Below: In brighter skies the town of Bastogne receives an air drop.

Americans had so recently opened, he could concentrate on taking the town. Such was the commitment to Hitler's insistence that Bastogne must be taken, that now much of 1st SS Panzer had been hurried to this sector and the 'Führer' division was threatening to break American lines at Villers-la-Bonne-Eau, just five miles south of the town centre.

Fierce fighting ensued as German artillery tried to support an uncertain tank advance that quickly came under fire from the American defensive cordon, and there was much jockeying for advantage as the firepower of both sides was directed onto the same segment of the defensive ring. Poor visibility prevented effective use of artillery, and piecemeal advances brought a state of confusion with every report of German units breaking the American line being countered by another saying that no progress was being made and that men and vehicles were being lost. Even a partial lifting of the persistent mists did not help clarify the tangled battle positions.

To the west of the town German moves on Sibret via Chenogne were initially hindered by dense fog but forced the Americans back before it lifted. Thereafter, however, repeated small thrusts and stout defence continued to thwart the German troops and as the year ended there was little doubt that the Americans were easing the pressure on Bastogne rather than the Germans regaining their encirclement.

New Year's Eve saw the troops at Bastogne and Wiltz still engaged in tough fighting at close quarters with heavy loss of life on both sides. At the foot of Hill 490 just south of Wiltz a particularly tough infantry action was resolved in the Americans' favour when they called for an artillery barrage on their own position.

As if in contemplation of its own death-throes, Sixth Panzer Army had made a final attempt on the American defences between the Salm and the Ourthe when, having accepted the loss of Manhay and Grandemenil, one of its dispersed units became involved in skirmishes around Sadzot and Briscol. This area of steep valleys and rugged hills caused communication difficulties and confusion for both sides, and only a fierce assault by paratroops and a night attack behind a creeping barrage of star shells restored the situation in the Americans' favour. This was the last the Ardennes saw of Sixth Panzer Army as an attacking force; Model quickly ordered it into defensive mode and removed its usable armour, an undignified end of offensive action for Sepp Dietrich.

An exchange of letters at the year's end between Eisenhower and Montgomery cleared the air by means of the former enforcing his views about the way in which the Allied war should be fought and commanded and the latter, somewhat meekly, reassuring the Supreme Commander of his complete support and admitting that he was surely not as aware of the situation across the whole theatre as the American.

Meanwhile, Hitler was disclosing the plans for Operation 'Nordwind' to Otto Skorzeny and confirming that the Ardennes would remain a battle-field over which the Reich forces would be victorious despite recent setbacks. His rhetoric at this time remained upbeat and determined, but, as ever, he chose which facts should be noted and which ignored. All the pleading that firm defence east of Bastogne would still leave his forces farther west than they had been at the outset of 'Wacht am Rhein' was never likely to satisfy the man who was bored when defending. Elsewhere, we now know, General Kurt Student was disclosing to a select number of the sad remnant of von der Heydte's team who had survived the Ardennes drop that plans were afoot to assassinate Churchill, Roosevelt and Stalin at an upcoming summit meeting in Yalta, and that they would be involved.

As the year came to its end, Hitler broadcast a rabid '*cri de coeur*' to mark the beginning of 1945 and, as he put it, a time when 'we shall fulfil our duty faithfully and unshakeably in the New Year too, in the firm belief that the hour will strike when victory will ultimately come to him who is most worthy of it, the Greater German Reich!' He had earlier spoken of the people being 'resolved to fight the war to victory' and of Germany rising 'like a phoenix from its ruined cities'. He was marking the launch of the New Year and of 'Nordwind'; in the opening minutes of 1945, eight German divisions dashed forward from their West Wall positions into northern Alsace to tackle Seventh Army.

1–8 JANUARY 1945

As the new Operation began, other initiatives were started including Operation 'Bodenplatte' in which, on the morning of 1 January, sixteen Allied airfields in Holland and Belgium and one in France were attacked by the Luftwaffe with about 750 single-engined fighters, many of which were piloted by inexperienced men some of whom had not been briefed and were very vague as to their targets. Each group of aircraft was allotted two Ju-88s as navigators but these did not cross into Allied territory. Strict radio silence was observed and the Allied pilots and airfield personnel were taken unawares. The action lasted less than three hours, but accounted for 134 Allied aircraft with a further 62 damaged beyond unit repair. The cost to the Germans was 220 aircraft with their pilots for little long-term value. Afterwards, Allied and German claims in terms of numbers were grossly inflated.

The Führer's mood was darkened further by fresh news from Bastogne. He may have been aware that the invitation to McAuliffe to surrender was already amusing news reporters in London and Paris, but now he was not prepared to take any more prevarication. Von Manteuffel was convinced that any thought of further advance was ridiculous and was pleading with Model for a full withdrawal to a line north and east of Bastogne through Noville, Houffalize and Vielsalm. Although surely understanding the logic of this, neither Model nor von Rundstedt had the authority to agree, and the latter must have been appalled at the haphazard state of German tactics driven, as they were, by mania rather than military strategy.

Railing at the veteran Prussian, Hitler ranted that no one would be excused from the failure to take Bastogne … it must be taken, no matter at what cost in German lives. Von Rundstedt transmitted the nonsensical message to Model who instantly discounted the detail of Hitler's directive and asked that he be allowed to attack with 9th Panzer, 12th SS Panzer and the Führer Escort Brigade from the north, north-east and east respectively. The alternative plan was agreed to.

By 3 January the two American armies and one British corps were ready to re-impose their superiority across the Ardennes; they had staunched the flow from the 'bloody nose' Hitler's 'Wacht am Rhein' had given them and were ready to

Opposite page:
101st Airborne
Division troops dig
their buddies out of a
bombed building in
Bastogne.

exact revenge. Even Bernard Montgomery, having used his self-imposed pause to re-equip and re-energise his forces, was eager to chase the enemy back into its own country.

Against an early morning backcloth of fog and icy rain, First Army swept forward against the middle of the Bulge on its northern side. Infantry regiments of 75th and 84th Divisions accompanied tanks of 2nd Armored Division to the west of the Liège–Manhay road, 3rd Armored was joined by infantry regiments of 83rd Division in a move to the east of that route, and more units of 83rd Division formed a second wave. It has been suggested that, having waited for Montgomery and seen several days without any forward offensives, the Allied forces, and their commanders, were unduly confident about the ease at which the Germans would give ground when faced with this sharp riposte. Certainly those seeing 'live' action for the first time may have been forgiven for thinking this, but those who had retreated from forward positions close to the German West Wall had recent experience of the determination of the German soldier. They shouldn't have expected an easy fight and they were not to get one.

The weather was dreadful. Where roads were passable they were treacherous, and conditions prevented Allied fighter-bombers supporting their fellows on the ground. Pace was excruciatingly slow when it needed to be rapid, the battle-zone murky when it needed to be clear. As a result, where German forces might have been forced by fighter-bombers to withdraw, they were very ready to fight and further encouraged when seeing the slow pace of the enemy. The German infantryman was more at home in the dreadful weather and Allied

Below: A knocked-out Panther stands as mute testament to effective Allied firepower.

euphoria at the prospect of counter-attack was draining away as vehicles became stuck, orders had to be modified and the enemy became ever more reluctant to give ground. The terrain over which Montgomery's units were advancing was not ideal: thick wooded hills and gorges with line of fire visibility often only a few yards, all made worse by icy roads upon which fell persistent snow blizzards. Defenders of such territory had all the benefits. The commanders, particularly the noted pacemen such as Patton, were frustrated and the prospect of the advance becoming stillborn was very real.

So it was that the second and third days of the Allied initiative brought mostly stagnation and despair, as well as a great deal of hard fighting. In modern parlance the conflict was coming down to 'who wanted it more' and, in this respect, the Americans – all fighting thousands of miles from home, many of whom had fought hard to gain their foothold in France but had thereafter become accustomed to unfettered progress, might be expected to crack first. The simple necessities of food supply, the ability to dig-in if necessary, and the prompt provision of medical treatment were all prejudiced by the dreadful conditions. If the final fight for the Ardennes was to be a battle of wills among the infantry units of the combatants, who would emerge as victors?

With Patton himself stating that the war could still be lost, the battle for Bastogne still raging, and Hitler determined that his 'last stand' should produce a victory of some sort, the situation was on a knife-edge.

The next 72 hours saw a dramatic change. The Allied forces proved up to the task, showing a rampant determination to win every tussle, take every inch of disputed ground and employ effective tactics in the midst of fierce battle. Rested Allied forces had energy, their opponents had seen their impetus stopped and now faced the prospect of wretched defeat. Fortunes turned, advances continued, ground was taken. And while the next days would continue to see hard action, the campaign was all but won. Hitler accepted that Model must withdraw east of Houffalize if he were not to lose irreplaceable men and armour.

Adolf Hitler had bowed to the inevitable. In his Berlin bunker he had agreed to a substantial withdrawal that was not a temporary move and no sooner had that message reached the front lines than those on the Allied front lines witnessed panzer units turning round and hurrying east to avoid being enclosed by the joyful push their enemy was bound to launch.

9 JANUARY ONWARDS
THE BITER BITTEN

Now the Americans increased their pace. Men of First Army hurried towards Houffalize, Patton approached the town from the opposite direction and the embattled Hill 490 was finally taken as 90th Division attacked towards Wiltz and St-Vith. Some German units were caught after modest resistance and by 12 January almost15,000 German troops had been cut-off by moves from 90th, 6th Armored and 35th Divisions between Bastogne and Wiltz. This ended the battle for Bastogne.

By 13 January more Allied troops were busy 'clearing' the Ardennes. Houffalize was effectively encircled with Patton manoeuvring to launch a fresh attack from the west and Collins, with VII Corps, close to the north of the town. Matthew Ridgway's XVIII Corps was fully involved elsewhere, driving south past Stavelot to Vielsalm and Salmchâteau and on to the northern perimeter of the retreating German forces. Within another 48 hours 84th and 2nd Armored Divisions were across the Amblève from Houffalize and by the 16th First and Third Armies had linked up.

Patton, having shed his sombre mood of the past week, was again the ener- getic cheerful leader. He sent some of his forces to tackle Wiltz and St-Vith, and XX Corps' 4th, 5th and 80th Divisions to reinforce the stubborn battle in the Echternach and Diekirch region. Now even the heaviest snowfalls of the winter could not hold back the Allied advance, and only isolated and abandoned rear- guard defensive units made up of young boys and old men were left to delay the Americans as they pursued retreating groups of Dietrich and von Manteuffel's armies. Airborne attacks added to the Germans' misery as those American troops driven from the Ardennes towns just a few weeks before, such as Robert Hasbrouck's 7th Armored Division, returned to recapture their old locations.

The town of St-Vith was re-occupied on 23 January – by the man who had had to abandon it on 17 December, Bruce Clarke. The great German Army that had caused such havoc a short while ago was now reduced to a few hundred hapless snipers left behind by retreating commanders to take such frail revenge as they could on the reoccupying Americans. The fleeing Germans were not having an easy time; strafing fighter-bombers accounted for more than 1,000 vehicles.

Below: The US 7th Armored Division marches into St-Vith.

The defeated legions were a sorry sight indeed. Few could get back quickly to the 'safety' of the homeland because so much of their motorised transport, armoured or otherwise, lay far behind them abandoned or destroyed. With each mile that their tired limbs and damaged bodies could carry them, they came closer to the moment when they must show themselves to their countrymen as a destroyed and

THE GERMAN ARMY RETREATS

Map labels:

0 Miles 5

To Liége

To La Gleize

XVIII CORPS (Ridgway)

VII CORPS (Collins)

R. Ambiève

Stavelot

Trois Ponts

R. Salm

Grandménil

Manhay

Baraque de Fraiture

Vielsalm

82 Abn Div

2 Armd Div

84 Inf Div

Parker's Crossroads

Salmchâteau

Hotton

Bihain

83 Inf Div

Marche

Verdenne

R. Ourthe

Marcouray

3 Armd Div

Chérain

Bouvigny

53 British Div

La Roche

To St-Vith

Achouffe

Mont

FIFTH PANZER ARMY

87 Inf Div

Engreux

11 Armd Div

Noville

St. Hubert

17 Abn Div

6 Armd Div

Bastogne

Wiltz

35 Inf Div

VIII CORPS (Middleton)

III CORPS (Millikin)

German Line

Neufchâteau

Allied Advances

115

demoralised force, albeit the same men the leader of their nation had assured everyone would bring fresh glory to their land. Now they had only misery and horror, diseased and mangled bodies, stories of great loss of life and absolute failure.

For this is how 'Wacht am Rhein' was ending ... as complete and utter failure. However close the call had been, how near the Germans had got to crossing the River Meuse, whatever disagreement in Allied command had been proven and however tenuous the resolve of the individual Allied soldier might have been at times, Adolf Hitler's final offensive act had ended in wretched loss. The Battle of the Bulge, Hitler's last military adventure, was over. By the time buds had turned to blossom on the now snow-covered trees and hedgerows, the Führer would have committed suicide and the German nation would have surrendered.

US 4th Armored
Division personnel
look on as German
prisoners pass by.

6

ASSESSMENT

The Battle of the Bulge is rightly celebrated as a triumphant battle within a successful war and, once the German attacks were under way, most of the Allied decision-making was up to the mark. That the Ardennes Offensive was sufficiently forceful and threatening to provoke the most concentrated deployment of US land forces in the 1939–45 conflict, is testament to the determination shown by Adolf Hitler and the manner in which his dictates were loyally carried out until the point where they were no longer valid. But the man who had so criticised the tactics and outcome of the First World War, left his country in a far worse state than had the Kaiser and his generals.

Over-confidence is always dangerous in a competitive environment; even more so when it has little or no justification. Hitler never had a chance of achieving his intended breakthrough along his treasured Ardennes route, though he did not lose the war because he lost the Ardennes Offensive. Did he lose this battle or did the Allies win it? We have seen the multiple elements which formed his decision to launch his offensive: first they were personal – those of ego, pride and desperation; secondly they were political and national – he could not contemplate a German defeat; thirdly he deemed them feasible, despite the parlous state of the war at that time, because he felt that he had been able to create the manpower and weaponry that *his* theory suggested would make it all workable. He could not be sure that the advanced weaponry he craved would ever arrive in time to turn the war his way, but he could be absolutely certain that Eisenhower and his Allied forces would not stay in their current locations for long; nor would the Soviet Army simply sit tight in their currently threatening positions.

As a national leader he constantly over-estimated his attributes as a military commander, and the ability of his war machine to see him through to victory. He overruled finer military minds than his, showing little or no military discretion where others would have used theirs. His quixotic fixation on thrusting through the Ardennes for a second time was evidence of strategy built on fanciful notions and immature thinking where a military brain of greater power would have perhaps seen the route as one ideal for a diversionary attack ahead of the real thing at a more suitable location. Even Hitler, with his impatience with the detail of strategy, must have appreciated the role that the Luftwaffe had played in 1940 and realised that his air force was in no position to provide a repeat performance now.

But at least he never wavered in his decision to go with the Ardennes drive, though even this was not entirely typical for he was a serial vacillator, as evidenced when delaying the von Manstein plan on no fewer than 29 occasions.

Because he ran the war dictatorially, accepted no criticism, listened to no advice and did not learn from errors, Hitler opened up too many fronts – after he himself had warned of the dangers of doing so – and regularly set an oppo-

Opposite page: An aerial view of St-Vith taken on 24 January 1945.

site track to that which military strategy suggested was best – heading for the oil and industry to the south rather than committing all on the vital prize of Moscow, yet fighting long and hard for Stalingrad which was a symbolic trophy rather than a necessity. It is indicative of the man that he felt he could direct his Army's countering of the street-fighting tactics of the Red Army in that city by plotting the action on a large-scale map hundreds of miles away.

The soldier in the ranks had only seen his Führer at rallies; he was the man who said, 'I only want to be the foremost soldier in the Third Reich. I wear the uniform with pride', but who, well before the Ardennes, had long since ceased to visit his fighting men in the field.

His generals had to obey him or risk demotion or worse, and those who risked confronting him were few. Had he not excluded the employment of any officers with any vestige of involvement in the July bomb plot, we might have seen Rommel opposing Montgomery again, and perhaps less dithering from the reluctant von Rundstedt and the overwhelmed Model. And there was Guderian, who at least had been associated with similar campaigns, but would probably have added little, involved with the preliminary discussions about the plan and then side-lined.

Had Hitler not declared war on the USA when he did, it would no doubt have happened in due course but perhaps it was the ultimate folly and presumption to believe, from that declaration until the Ardennes action was well under way, that the Americans would not have the courage for the fight once they had encountered their first reverse. The Allied forces in the Ardennes, and all along the north-west Europe front, were a match for Hitler's hastily created mongrel forces in the winter of 1944–5

The German leader was acting like a caged beast at this time – or, rather, a beast being forced back towards the open door of a cage in which it is to be held captive – and such an animal is liable to snap back at those who make a threatening approach and may continue such histrionics long after its position is transparently hopeless. It goes against animal instincts to rest and gather strength, allow some threats and advances, and then put all your effort into one energy-fuelled attempt at attack or escape, yet this is what the Ardennes seems to have been. Hitler had insufficient skilled and experienced forces, too little weaponry and an inadequate grasp on reality, at least in the eyes of his critics. And so he waited, and waited. We have seen that he had been considering an autumn/winter counter for some months and that, while the loss of Antwerp was a wretched business for him, the delay by the Allies in making it a secure and usable port had given him a window of opportunity.

Just as he was about to be pushed back into the 'cage' of abject defeat, he reached for the bars of the door and started to kick out. This is what the Ardennes battle was; it was Hitler 'kicking out' at those who would capture him. However foolhardy the Ardennes adventure might have been, Hitler certainly chose the right time to attempt the strategy, if right time there could ever have been. As his captors paused to check that they had the chains and padlock, he lashed out one last time.

And what of the Allies? We know that Bradley had read his history, and probably should have allowed his knowledge of the 1940 German thrust through the Ardennes to feature more acutely in his situation assessments, but he was not the guilty party in allowing the Germans a foothold in their advance. There is no doubt whatsoever that Eisenhower reacted promptly and effectively once the size and scope of the attack had been absorbed, but should he have been surprised at all and should he and his generals have left the Ardennes so poorly defended? The answer to both of these questions is 'No', but with qualifications.

It is argued in defence colleges around the world that an advancing force is at its most vulnerable when it believes that the enemy is incapable of effective counter-attack; it is the caged animal syndrome again. The British were perhaps the most likely to urge caution at this point in the drive to and across the German border for they had witnessed the Blitzkrieg years at first hand and had been driven back by German forces before; the Americans, on the other hand, were novices and the more likely to assume their successes up to this point would continue. But this theoretical argument is annulled by the circumstances of the war and the political situation away from the front line.

Churchill wanted the war done with before the national elections, and had become despondent by the delays at Antwerp and the failure at Arnhem; Roosevelt was showing great faith in Eisenhower and the American forces fighting 'on a foreign field' in such large numbers for the first time. The two leaders both had an eye to the duplicity of Stalin, after his successful repulsion of German forces in the east, and on the efforts of the Japanese in the Pacific. In effect, both leaders, and therefore the majority in the nations they served, were urging the speediest conclusion to the European war by the complete defeat of Hitler and the Third Reich; they felt the commanders in the field were aware of this requirement and trusted them to complete the task as promptly as possible.

With this in mind, could Eisenhower have tested the West Wall defences more substantially and earlier? Did he wait longer than necessary to unleash Montgomery in the north and Patton in the south? And, if he was determined to wait until the forward movement could be more concerted and thorough, should he have left his wide front as weakly defended in its centre as he did?

The answer to the latter point surely comes down to three understandable considerations. First, to be ready to strike forward again into German territory, the majority of his forces were best positioned to the north and south of the Ardennes; secondly, it was against all strategic logic for the Allies or their opponents to undertake any action through the Ardennes, especially at this time of year; thirdly, of all the sectors of the front line where troops new to the area or resting from recent actions could be positioned, the Ardennes was the most suitable. Furthermore, Eisenhower was lulled into a sense of false security by the erroneous reports from his own Intelligence network.

We have shown that the Allies noticed the German build-up but assumed it to be part of moves to strengthen the West Wall defences, but the routes these forces were following as they moved farther west were taking them directly towards the Ardennes rather than elsewhere; the failure to interpret the German moves was partly due to the relative paucity of this Intelligence but those responsible for assessing the data received did not perform at their best. Perhaps, even if Bradley knew of 1940, too few of the American Intelligence officers did. Fundamentally, the Allied commanders considered the Ardennes to be a 'dormant' region of the front and did not consider that the enemy's view might differ from their own.

It is a great testament to German organisation that they could first create a new reserve in such a short time, then produce aircraft and weaponry to support them. The manpower found may have been of suspect quality but it was produced; a quarter of a million men ready to fight. Albert Speer drove German industry until it could work no faster, where every rivet was put into the war effort and each piece of valuable metal used and re-used to produce planes, armour and ammunition. Those who sweated the long hours in factories and the many cajoled into military service deserved better use of their work and time.

Below: Albert Speer worked wonders to keep German manufacturers working for the war effort, but even he could not produce enough armour and ammunition to win in the Ardennes.

Certainly his offensive saw Adolf Hitler suffer for having opened up so many fronts, especially in Russia. Having a dread and loathing of defeat and reversal, the Führer could not bring himself to make the sacrifices of territory that would have freed good quality fighting men and their equipment. But Hitler certainly surprised his enemy. Just as von Rundstedt had predicted, the bravado that caused him to decide on the Ardennes was a master stroke in many ways, if driven by hopeless optimism. Considering his lack of involvement in the scheme, the veteran field marshal's summary of the plan was accurate and pertinent for not only did he know he could not shore up the West Wall defences sufficiently to stop the Allied advance, but also he was firm in his prediction that

'Wacht am Rhein' would prove little more than an irritant, a minor hindrance to such a rampant opponent. The expectation of reaching the Meuse, and crossing it, in such a short time was, von Rundstedt knew, vital but impossible.

The best a military commander can hope for in a long and diverse war is to be able to react to a surprise attack or counter-attack efficiently since to expect to avoid such instances is either foolish, over-confident or over-reliant on the blessing of good luck. When the Germans launched the first fusillade of shells at the American forces on the misty, dull dawn of 16 December 1944, they achieved undiluted surprise, but as it turned out they could not utilise it as they should have done and were elsewhere prevented from doing so by the tough resistance of the units at the front, and then by Eisenhower's swift tactical riposte. Here, the Allied cause was well served by a clear, decisive mind and then the fast response to the instructions it issued.

The Ardennes region, as we have seen, was criss-crossed by minor roads and tracks, but only a handful of worthwhile, serviceable thoroughfares. It was vital that the Allies hold the towns at the junctions of these main routes, and just as important that the Germans take them. Hence, St-Vith and Bastogne became focal points for both sides, with the American efforts at both locations proving decisive in delaying, then defeating, the enemy's ambitions; the towns were the rocks that the tide of German advance could sweep around but not easily dislodge.

Once the German drive had been delayed and diverted, the mists and low cloud that had arrived 'on cue' to assist the early attacking moves evaporated for long enough to allow Allied air power to show its superiority, and with this any remaining hopes of further German progress could be forgotten. Although both air forces were active only one was ever going to dominate; the fighters of the Ninth Army Air Force were better equipped, better flown and more effective. Many German supply lines were severed and land armour destroyed at a whim and, though the Allies lost aircraft in some numbers, this was the end of the Luftwaffe as a significant attacking threat.

Hitler had 'grasped the straw' of surprise; it was the only worthwhile advantage he could claim. His Ardennes Offensive was a fool's philosophy that ill-served his country, not least in that it misused and abused both its willing fighting men and its resourceful industrial workers; it denuded the nation of personnel and *matériel* that might have been used in defence while negotiations to end to the war were undertaken. It is ironic that having driven his subordinates to produce ammunition and weaponry, and got huge numbers of men to the attack line without alerting the opposition, Hitler's plan foundered, in part at least, on relatively small logistical oversights and errors such as tanks arriving at river crossings before the arrival of the pontoons that would carry them across, or their own land-mines not being cleared after earlier withdrawals and thus accounting for their own vehicles, or of the inability of the foreign labour pressed into manning horse-drawn supply units to understand orders barked at them in German.

There were other errors and omissions. Troops brought forward in response to demands from battlefield commanders often had to travel great distances although other groups that were nearer could have been deployed, and flanks of the main salients were allowed to become cluttered and slow-moving in comparison. But, above all, the main error on the part of Hitler and Jodl, once the offensive was under way, was to fail to give added support to von Manteuffel when Dietrich was seen to be stalled.

At the very top of the guilt league, Adolf Hitler completely under-estimated the enemy. It was the height of foolishness to believe he was fighting the same enemy that he had destroyed in the same region in 1940. This was as transparently obvious then as it is now with all the value of hindsight.

We have discussed Hitler's physical and mental state at the end of 1944 and acknowledged that his weak grasp of military strategy was solely aligned with attacking action. He was never going to defend at his borders nor was he going to negotiate; it was just not something he had ever done. Nevertheless, his generals

were right, these were his two worth while options and had he given von Rundstedt the men and *matériel* to defend the Rhine, instead of throwing them at the last gasp surprise attack in the Ardennes, he would have acted in the better interests of his countrymen, though certainly not prevented them from coming second.

But this is not the way of dictators; they do not go quietly, they do not acquiesce in their own downfall or submit to routine prosecution of any sins or judgement of poor performance. Hitler can only claim to have delayed the inevitable and brought to an unexpected battle the largest number of American land forces seen up to that time. The Allied losses were substantial, but their victory eased their path to Berlin. Hitler, from a deteriorating mind, conjured up an unsophisticated counter-offensive at the soft centre of the enemy line. He delayed the Allies by no more than six weeks; this was the sum total of his planning, ranting and dictates. He lost more than 100,000 men who could have defended their country more stoutly. Because of it, however, the man lost his country and his people, and he took his own life just a few months later to avoid having to answer for these failures.

Below: US Ninth Army Air Force fighter-bombers inflicted this carnage in the Houffalize area.

7
CONCLUSION

The Ardennes Offensive and the Battle of the Bulge represented all the facets of a major war strategy within a small sector of north-western Europe during a few days in the winter of 1944–5. The Allies were never going to lose the European war because of this counter-move by Hitler, but they were caused to exercise every type of military activity to defeat a determined enemy and, because of these facts, it is a subject that will always engage the attention of history and military students.

The American forces, brought to Europe to support the taking of the battle back to the Germans, represented that country's greatest commitment to an overseas war at that point, and they lost many fine men in the process. As the advance from the Normandy beaches to Paris and on to the German border had been a good example of military alliance, so the Ardennes featured American and some British forces in concert, but this was principally an American victory and one of which they are rightly proud. No wars are fought with perfect strategies, not every commander gets his tactics right and many a foot soldier quakes at the thought of his first battle, so it is disingenuous to be too critical of a force which, to a large degree, was learning as it fought.

Below: Much of the German supply transport was horse-drawn and vulnerable to air and ground attack.

SELECT BIBLIOGRAPHY

Arnold, James. *The Battle of the Bulge*. Osprey, 1992

Baudot, M., et al. *The Historical Encyclopedia Of World War Two*. Facts on File, 1989

Barnett, Correlli (ed.). *Hitler's Generals*. Weidenfeld & Nicholson, 1989

Cole, Hugh. *The Ardennes: The Battle of The Bulge*. Konecky & Konecky, 2000

Crookenden, Napier. *The Battle of the Bulge*. Ian Allan, 1978

Dear, I. C. B. (ed). *The Oxford Companion to the Second World War*. Oxford University Press, 1995

Eisenhower, J. D. *The Bitter Woods*. Birlinn, 1969

Essame, H. *The Battle for Germany*. Batsford, 1969

Lewin, Ronald. *Montgomery as Military Commander*. Batsford, 1971

McDonald, Charles. *The Battle of the Bulge*. Phoenix, 1984

Parker, Danny S. *The Battle of the Bulge*. Greenhill, 1999

Sixsmith, E. K. G. *Eisenhower as Military Commander*. Batsford, 1973

Snyder, Louis. *The Encyclopedia of the Third Reich*. Blandford, 1989

Strawson, John. *The Battle for the Ardennes*. Batsford

Toland, John. *The Battle of the Bulge*. Muller, 1959

Whiting, Charles. *The Battle of the Bulge*. Sutton, 1994

NOTES

1 Strawson, J. *The Battle for the Ardennes*.
2 Toland, J. *The Battle of the Bulge*
3 Essame, H. *The Battle for Germany*
4 Toland, J. *The Battle of the Bulge*
5 Strawson, J. *The Battle for the Ardennes*
6 Saunders, H. *Die Wacht am Rhein*
7 Cole, Hugh. *The Ardennes: The Battle of the Bulge*
8 Kurowski, Frank, ed. C. Barnett. *Hitler's Generals*
9 Toland, J. *The Battle of the Bulge*
10 Blumenson, M. in *Armor*
11 Lewin, R. *Montgomery as a Military Commander*

INDEX